Coping with Behavioral Addictions

I0113490

The Gambling Addiction Workbook

Information, Assessments, and Tools for Managing Life with a Behavioral Addiction

Ester R.A. Leutenberg and John J. Liptak, EdD

Whole Person Associates

101 West 2nd Street, Suite 203
Duluth, MN 55802-5004

800-247-6789

Books@WholePerson.com
WholePerson.com

The Gambling Addiction Workbook

Printed in the United States of America

Editorial Director: Jack Kosmach
Art Director: Mathew Pawlak
Cover Design: Adam Sippola
Editor: Peg Johnson

Library of Congress Control Number: 2020945964
ISBN:978-1-57025-362-1

From the co-authors, Ester and John
Our gratitude, thanks, and appreciation
to the following professionals:

❦ ○ ❧

Editorial Directors – Jack Kosmach & Peg Johnson

Editor and Life-long Teacher – Eileen Regen, MEd, CIE

Reviewers – Carol Butler Cooper, MS Ed, RN, C and Niki Tilicki, MA Ed

Proof-reader – Jay Leutenberg, CASA

Art Director – Mathew Pawlak

❦ ○ ❧

A Special Thank You
to
Whole Person Associates

for their interest in mental health issues.

Free PDF Download Available

To access your free PDF download of the assessment tools
and all of the reproducible activities in this workbook, go to:
https://WholePerson.com/store/TheGamblingAddictionWorkbook5964.html

© 2021 WHOLE PERSON ASSOCIATES, 101 WEST 2ND STREET, SUITE 203, DULUTH MN 55802 • 800-247-6789 • WHOLEPERSON.COM

Understanding Behavioral Addictions

There are many types of addictions. The addictions that have been talked about most have been substance abuse addictions. However, behavioral addictions can occur that take the same form as a physical dependence on substances. According to the American Addiction Centers (2019):

> ...it is the compulsive nature of the behavior that is often indicative of a behavioral addiction, or process addiction, in an individual. The compulsion to continually engage in an activity or behavior despite the negative impact on the person's ability to remain mentally and/or physically healthy and functional in the home and community defines behavioral addiction. The person may find the behavior rewarding psychologically or get a "high" while engaged in the activity but may later feel guilt, remorse, or even overwhelmed by the consequences of that continued choice. Unfortunately, as is common for all who struggle with addiction, people living with behavioral addictions are unable to stop engaging in the behavior for any length of time without treatment and intervention.
>
> People are increasingly experiencing non-substance behavioral addictions and the diminished control over the behaviors they cause. No longer categorized as impulse disorders, behavioral addictions are now being viewed as true addictions much like substance abuse.

~American Addiction Centers

The National Institute of Health (2010) states:

Growing evidence suggests that behavioral addictions often resemble substance addictions in many ways, including natural history, phenomenology, tolerance, comorbidity, overlapping genetic contribution, neurobiological mechanisms, and response to treatment.

> The concept of addiction, for years used to indicate the use of psychotropic substances, is now being applied to describe a heterogeneous group of syndromes known as "behavioral addictions," "no-drug addictions," or "new addictions." Prevalence rates for such conditions are among the highest registered for mental disorders with social, cultural, and economic implications. Individual forms of behavioral addictions are linked by a series of psychopathological features that include: repetitive, persistent, and dysfunctional behaviors, loss of control over behavior in spite of the negative repercussions of the latter, compulsion to satisfy the need to implement the behavior, initial well-being produced by the behavior, craving, onset of tolerance, abstinence, and, ultimately, a progressive, significant impairment of overall individual functioning.

Grant, et al, 2010

Why Are They Called Behavioral Addictions?

Behavioral addictions constitute any maladaptive pattern of excessive behavior that manifests in physiological, psychological and cognitive symptoms such as:

- **Continuance:** continuing the behavior despite knowing that this activity is creating or exacerbating physical, psychological, and/or interpersonal problems.
- **Intention effects:** unable to stick to one's routine, as evidenced by exceeding the amount of time devoted to the behavior or consistently going beyond the intended amount.
- **Lack of control:** unsuccessful attempts to reduce the level of the behavior or cease it for a certain period of time.
- **Reduction in activities:** as a direct result of the behavior, social, familial, occupational and/or recreational activities occur less often or are stopped.
- **Time:** a great deal of time is spent preparing for, engaging in, and recovering from the behavior.
- **Tolerance:** increasing the amount of the behavior in order to feel the desired effect, being it a buzz or a sense of accomplishment.
- **Withdrawal:** in the absence of the behavior the person experiences negative effects such as anxiety, irritability, restlessness, and sleep problems.

Addiction to Gambling

Gambling addiction—also known as pathological gambling, compulsive gambling, or gambling disorder—is an impulse-control disorder. Compulsive gamblers struggle to control the impulse to gamble, even when it has negative consequences for them or their loved ones. They will tend to gamble whether they are winning, or losing, or broke, or ahead financially. They keep gambling regardless of the consequences, even when they know that the odds are against them or they cannot afford to lose. Gambling problems vary in intensity. People who are addicted can also have a gambling problem without being totally out of control. Gambling addiction or gambling disorder is defined as: persistent and recurring problematic gambling behavior that causes distress and impairs your overall livelihood.

It is important to remember that gambling is NOT just a financial problem. Some gamblers who are addicted do not have financial issues even though they may lose money gambling. Gambling is an emotional issue in which people feel the need to gamble to alleviate stress or because they feel a certain type of euphoria when they gamble. Gambling is an obsession that can take over one's life if allowed to go too far and can lead to the loss of relationships, jobs, education, and finances.

The desire to purchase lottery tickets, play slot machines, play online poker, and visit casinos are not necessarily signs of a gambling addiction. But when the desire to gamble becomes overwhelming to the point that people cannot stop thinking about it until they gamble on something, it may signal a need for help. Those who suffer from gambling addiction will continue to gamble despite negative financial, legal, relational, and social consequences.

Segal, Smith, Robinson, 2019

When gambling becomes a problem, it can push people to do things they would not normally do if they were not suffering from an addiction. Behavioral addictions like gambling can be difficult to manage (Holler, 2020). The pages of this workbook are filled with assessments, activities, and journaling exercises that can help your clients or students overcome a gambling addiction and teach them important skills aimed at helping them repair problems in their lives caused by gambling.

Gambling Disorder in the DSM-5

The latest edition of the Diagnostic and Statistical Manual of Mental Disorders (DSM-5) reconceptualized addictive behavior to include behavioral addictions akin to more traditional drug addictions. A profound change was made: Gambling Disorder (formerly pathological gambling) was reclassified as a behavioral addiction rather than a disorder of impulse control.

According to the DSM-5, gambling addiction is characterized by a persistent and recurrent gambling behavior that leads to personal distress and problems in social, occupational, or other areas of functioning. You may be suffering from this if you meet four or more of the following criteria during a 12-month period.

- A need to gamble with increasing amounts of money to feel excited.

- Restlessness or irritability when trying to restrict or cut back on gambling.

- Repeated unsuccessful attempts to control, stop, or reduce gambling behaviors.

- A mental preoccupation with gambling, such as thinking of ways to get gambling money or reliving past gambling experiences.

- Gambling to relieve stress.

- Returning to gambling after significant monetary losses, especially with the intention of gaining back losses.

- Lying to conceal gambling activity, involvement, or debts.

- Jeopardizing relationships, jobs, or education for the sake of gambling.

- Relying on others to get out of desperate financial situations caused by gambling.

Gambling can be a behavioral addiction that can be effectively treated using a range of cognitive and behavioral therapies.

© 2021 WHOLE PERSON ASSOCIATES, 101 WEST 2ND STREET, SUITE 203, DULUTH MN 55802 • 800-247-6789 • WHOLEPERSON.COM

Potential Signs of Gambling Addiction

One can also have a gambling issue without being totally out of control. Problem gambling is any gambling behavior that disrupts the various aspects of your life. If one is preoccupied with gambling, spending more and more time and money on it, chasing losses, or gambling despite serious consequences, one has a gambling problem. As the intensity of the gambling problem increases, the person is at risk to become addicted to gambling.

Holler, 2020

THE FOLLOWING BEHAVIORS ARE POTENTIAL SIGNS OF GAMBLING ADDICTION:

Those with a mild gambling addiction may exhibit <u>four or five</u> of these behaviors, while those with a moderately severe gambling addiction may exhibit <u>six or seven</u> of these behaviors. People who suffer from severe gambling addiction will often exhibit all of the behaviors.

Risk factors

People can enjoy playing cards and placing an occasional wager while never developing a gambling problem or addiction. With this in mind, GamblingAddiction.com helps identify certain factors that are often associated with gambling addictions:

- People with gambling addictions often have substance abuse problems, personality disorders, depression, or anxiety.

- Gambling addictions are more common in younger and middle-aged people.

- Gambling addictions are more common in men than women.

- Gambling addictions are more common in people who have been abused or traumatized.

- Family members and friends who have a gambling problem can be influential.

- People with gambling addictions often feel bored or lonely.

- People with gambling addictions usually have a history of risk-taking or impulsive behavior.

- People with gambling addictions share certain personality characteristics like competitiveness, impulsiveness, and restlessness.

Negative Effects of Gambling Addiction

Gambling addiction can produce many more negative effects than just financial hardship. An addiction to gambling can affect a person's physical health, mental health, and social functioning, and can also lead to the loss of important relationships with friends and family members. People who are experiencing a gambling addiction may also suffer a decline in work productivity, school performance, and feel restless and bored with other areas of life that do not involve gambling.

Those who from have a gambling addiction tend to suffer from higher rates of poor general health than those who do not have a gambling addiction. Many who suffer from gambling addiction also tend to experience distortions in thinking surrounding their addiction, such as superstitions, overconfidence, and a sense of power over the outcome of chance events.

Problem Gambling Can Affect People in Many Ways

- A decline in performance at work or school.
- A higher risk for drug or alcohol abuse.
- Behavior problems in the children of problem gamblers.
- Depression, anxiety, and other mental health disorders.
- Domestic violence and child abuse in families.
- Financial problems including high debt, poverty, stealing, or bankruptcy.
- Legal troubles, including arrests for theft or prostitution.
- Loss of relationships with friends and family.
- Suicidal thoughts, attempts, or the act of suicide.

Withdrawal

Gambling addiction signs often include withdrawal when one goes without gambling behaviors. Like any other true addiction withdrawal, these may include such symptoms such as:

- Anxiety
- Grumpiness
- Headaches
- Depression
- Restlessness
- Sleep issues
- Cravings
- Agitation
- Irritability

Although the mental and emotional withdrawal symptoms may be intense, they are a necessary aspect of the recovery process. Withdrawal is different for every person, but most people will exhibit some of the symptoms identified above.

© 2021 WHOLE PERSON ASSOCIATES, 101 WEST 2ND STREET, SUITE 203, DULUTH MN 55802 • 800-247-6789 • WHOLEPERSON.COM

Using This Workbook

The purpose of *The Gambling Addiction Workbook* is to provide helping professionals with cognitive and behavioral assessments, tools, and exercises that can be utilized to treat the root psychological causes of a gambling addiction. It is designed to help people identify and change negative, unhealthy thoughts and behaviors that may have led to a gambling addiction. The activities contained in this workbook can help participants identify their triggers that lead to gambling and teach them ways to overcome and manage those triggers.

The Gambling Addiction Workbook **will help participants to:**

- Recognize that they are experiencing an addiction problem.
- Reflect and become aware of the behaviors that were part of and arose from the addiction.
- Build self-esteem in positive capabilities outside of gambling.
- Understand the triggers for preoccupation with gambling.
- Develop greater self-acceptance and the ability to change ineffective behaviors.
- Understand recurring patterns that indicate a gambling disorder.
- Learn ways to live a new life without the need to gamble.

The Gambling Addiction Workbook is a practical tool for therapists, counselors, and helping professionals in their work with people suffering with behavioral addictions. Depending on the role of the person using this workbook and the specific group's or individual's needs, the modules can be used either individually or as part of an integrated curriculum. The facilitator may choose to administer one of the activities to a group or administer some of the assessments over one or more days as a workshop.

Confidentiality When Completing Activity Handouts

Participants will see the words "NAME CODES" on some of the activities in the modules. Instruct participants that when writing or speaking about anyone, they should use name codes to preserve privacy and anonymity. These codes will allow participants to explore their feelings without hurting anyone's feelings or fearing gossip, harm or retribution. For example, a friend named Jack who **W**orks **O**ut **D**aily might be assigned a name code of **W.O.D.** for a particular exercise. In order to protect others' identities, they will not use people's actual names or initials, just NAME CODES.

The Five Modules

This workbook contains five separate modules of activity-based handouts that will help participants learn more about themselves and about their addiction to gambling. These modules serve as avenues for self-reflection and group experiences revolving around topics of importance in the lives of the participants in the group.

The activities in this workbook are user-friendly and varied to provide a comprehensive method of analyzing, strengthening, and developing characteristics, skills, and attitudes for overcoming an addiction to gambling.

The activities in this workbook are completely reproducible and can be photocopied and/or revised for direct participant use.

Module 1: My Gambling History

This module helps participants explore their gambling history by examining family traditions, signs of a gambling addiction, gambling habits, medical issues, social and emotional influencers, stressors that trigger the urge to gamble, and the plan for lasting change when addicted to gambling.

Module 2: Awareness of Gambling

This module helps participants explore awareness of their gambling problems by examining their destructive gambling patterns, the triggers that promote gambling, the emotions involved with gambling, the unrealistic thoughts that can promote gambling, and the destructive aspects of the denial of a gambling issue.

Module 3: Money Issues

This module helps participants examine the impact on their financial life by exploring the results of having to borrow and/or finance a gambling addiction, the ways they get their money, how much they typically spend, how a budget can help to reduce the urge to gamble, who enables them, and how they feed their gambling habit.

Module 4: Effects of Gambling

This module helps participants observe how gambling affects their life by investigating the effects of gambling on their occupational functioning, legal problems, financial difficulties, emotional issues, psychological problems, and relationships.

Module 5: Finding Healthy Alternatives

This module helps participants discover healthy ways to spend their time other than gambling by investigating healthy alternatives, managing their cravings, creating healthy habits, relying on supportive people, relaxing, helping others to help themselves, and developing hobbies to relieve boredom.

© 2021 WHOLE PERSON ASSOCIATES, 101 WEST 2ND STREET, SUITE 203, DULUTH MN 55802 • 800-247-6789 • WHOLEPERSON.COM

Different Types of Activity Handouts Included in this Workbook

Some of the various types of materials included in this reproducible workbook:

- **Action Plans** that assist participants in meeting the goals and objectives of treatment.

- **Assessments** that allow participants to explore their behavior. Often these assessments occur in pre-test and post-test formats to allow participants to track their progress.

- **Case Studies** which allow participants the opportunity to provide their thoughts pre-test about actual cases.

- **Drawing and Doodling** to unleash the power of the right side of the brain.

- **Educational Pages** that provide insights and tips related to the topic.

- **Group Activities** to encourage collaboration among participants and group thinking.

- **Journaling Activities** that can help participants clarify their thoughts and feelings, thus gaining helpful self-knowledge.

- **Positive Affirmations** that allow participants to create formidable affirmations that can be posted and repeated to oneself when impulses are felt.

- **Quotation Pages** that allow participants to reflect on many powerful quotes to see how they apply to their own life.

- **Rewards Pages** so that participants remember to reward themselves as they progress toward their goals.

- **Tables** which require participants to reflect on their lives in the past, understand themselves in the present, and react more effectively in the future.

References

American Addiction Centers (2019). Behavioral Addictions.
  https://americanaddictioncenters.org/behavioral-addictions

American Psychiatric Association (2018). Diagnostic and Statistical Manual of Mental Disorders (DSM–5).
  https://www.psychiatry.org/psychiatrists/practice/dsm

National Institute of Health (2010). Introduction to Behavioral Addictions.
  https://www.ncbi.nlm.nih.gov/pmc/articles/PMC3164585/

Segal, J., Smith, M., & Robinson, L. (2020). Gambling Addiction and Problem Gambling.
  https://www.helpguide.org/articles/addictions/gambling-addiction-and-problem-gambling.htm.

For the Participants
Three Critical Components for Your Success

1. CONFIDENTIALITY WHEN COMPLETING ACTIVITY HANDOUTS

You will see the words "NAME CODES" on some of the activities in the modules. When you are writing or speaking about anyone, use name codes for people to preserve privacy and anonymity. This will allow you to explore your feelings and stories without hurting anyone's feelings or fearing gossip, harm, or retribution. For example, a friend named Kathy who loves to read might be assigned a name code of L.T.R. for a particular exercise. In order to protect others' identities, you will not use people's actual names or initials, just NAME CODES that make sense to you.

2. HONESTY

In any type of therapeutic situation, honesty is critical in creating healing and lasting change. If you are not honest with yourself, with the group, and with the facilitator, you will not be helping yourself recover from your addiction. There will be times when you will want, or feel it is necessary, to reveal information that is uncomfortable for you. To get the most from this workbook, it becomes especially important that you do share.

Regarding a behavioral addiction, honesty contributes to recovery. When you are able to write about and share your own experience with others, it becomes cathartic and then a shared experience as opposed to an isolated one. Healing, sharing, and empathizing with others will help you to feel less isolated. Because honesty can directly influence your overall well-being, it is critical that you are honest when completing and responding to the assessments and activities that are included in this workbook.

3. DISCLOSURE

Disclosure in a group setting can be challenging. We all have things that we are not proud of and do not want to disclose. You may be concerned that if you disclose personal aspects of yourself or your experiences, you might not be accepted or understood, and people in the group will talk about you outside of the group. The motto of these sessions is "What is said in this room, stays in this room!" It is vital to be open and honest about your issues in order to get help with your addiction. You will help yourself by writing about and talking about your personal history and experiences. This workbook provides you with a venue for exploring various aspects of your life, and the group setting will allow you to explore your addiction in a safe and secure setting.

Table of Contents

(Continued on page xiv)

Table of Contents

Table of Contents

Gambling

My Gambling History

Name _____

Date _____

Gambling Addiction Signs Assessment
Introduction and Directions

Gambling can be highly destructive and can become an addiction if left unchecked. People with this addiction have difficulty resisting or controlling the impulse to gamble, in any form. An addiction to gambling has many disadvantages and consequences that include anxiety, depression, job loss, bankruptcy, loss of family and friends, and sometimes even suicide.

The *Gambling Addiction Signs Assessment* is designed to help you explore different types of signs that you may be suffering from an addiction to gambling. It contains statements that are divided into five categories.

Read each of the statements and decide how descriptive the statement is of you. In each of the choices listed, circle the number of your response on the line to the right of each statement.

In the following example, the circled 2 indicates the statement is LIKE the person completing the inventory:

	LIKE ME	UNLIKE ME
I. Related to my gambling ...		
I lie to hide the extent of my gambling.	(2)	1

This is not a test. Since there are no right or wrong answers, do not spend too much time thinking about your answers. Be sure to respond to every statement.

(Turn to the next page and begin.)

Gambling Addiction Signs Assessment (page 1)

Name _____ Date _____

This will only be accurate if you respond honestly. No one else needs to see this if you choose.

	LIKE ME	UNLIKE ME

I. Related to my gambling ...
I lie to hide the extent of my gambling. 2 1
I lie to my family. 2 1
I am preoccupied with gambling. 2 1
I am always thinking about the next time I can gamble. 2 1
I spend a lot of time gambling. 2 1
I try to hide my online gambling activities. 2 1

PRE-OCCUPATION – TOTAL = _____

	LIKE ME	UNLIKE ME

II. Related to my gambling ...
I have given up fun activities in order to gamble. 2 1
I have jeopardized intimate relationships due to gambling. 2 1
I no longer engage in family events in order to gamble. 2 1
I have hurt others who provide me with money to gamble. 2 1
I have compromised my job and career due to gambling. 2 1
I have lost friends due to my gambling. 2 1

LOSSES – TOTAL = _____

	LIKE ME	UNLIKE ME

III. Related to my gambling ...
I have repeatedly tried to gamble less. 2 1
I feel guilt and shame about gambling but cannot stop. 2 1
I have attempted to stop gambling without success. 2 1
I have cut down on gambling. 2 1
I have been unsuccessful in an attempt to stop gambling. 2 1
Others have tried to help me to stop gambling. 2 1

STOPPING – TOTAL = _____

Go to the next page for scoring assessment
results, profile interpretation, and individual descriptions

Gambling Addiction Signs Assessment (page 2)

Name _____ Date _____

This will only be accurate if you respond honestly. No one else needs to see this if you choose.

	LIKE ME	UNLIKE ME

IV. Related to my gambling ...

	LIKE ME	UNLIKE ME
I often experience desperate financial situations from gambling.	2	1
I have opened up new checking accounts to get money to gamble.	2	1
I have applied for new credit cards so I can gamble more.	2	1
I usually possess large amounts of cash that then disappear.	2	1
I borrow money for gambling.	2	1
I lie about my spending habits.	2	1

Money – TOTAL = _____

V. Related to my gambling ...

	LIKE ME	UNLIKE ME
I place increasingly large bets.	2	1
I lie to my family.	2	1
I have borrowed money from unwise sources.	2	1
I have stolen from others.	2	1
I risk my relationships in order to gamble.	2	1
I lose control of the amount of money I bet when I am gambling.	2	1

RISKS – TOTAL = _____

Scoring Directions

The Gambling Addiction Signs Scale is designed to measure the severity and the nature of the signs of gambling addiction you are currently experiencing.

For each of the five sections on the previous pages, count the scores you circled for each of the six items. Put that total on the line marked Total at the end of each section. Transfer your totals to the spaces below:

I.	**Preoccupation Total**	=	_____
II.	**Losses Total**	=	_____
III	**Stopping Total**	=	_____
IV.	**Money Total**	=	_____
V.	**Risks Total**	=	_____

Ways I Gamble

There are many different ways to gamble. People usually choose ways to gamble that fit their lifestyle, needs, and personality.

Following is a list of SOME of the ways people gamble.
Check off the ones that you do, how often, and why you like this gambling format.

☐ Video poker _Ex.: I play this when my wife goes to bed... she doesn't know I'm gambling this way!_

☐ Bingo_____

☐ Board games _____

☐ Card games _____

☐ Casino games_____

☐ Cell phone _____

☐ Cockfights _____

☐ Craps_____

☐ Dog fights_____

☐ Dog racing_____

☐ Fantasy sports leagues _____

☐ Fortnight and others _____

☐ Horse racing_____

☐ Illegal bookies_____

☐ Lottery_____

☐ Office pools_____

☐ Online casino_____

☐ Pai Gow _____

☐ Poker _____

☐ Pool tournaments_____

☐ Raffles _____

☐ Slot machines _____

☐ Sports betting_____

☐ Video poker _____

☐ Wagers on games of skill *(golf)* _____

☐ Other:_____

Reasons I Gamble

People usually start to gamble slowly and then become addicted to gambling. It is important to explore the various reasons that you gamble.

Below, identify the reasons that you gamble and how it helps and hurts you.

Reasons I Gamble	How It Helps Me	How It Hurts Me
Example: I feel the excitement or rush of adrenaline	*An energetic feeling that gives me strength and power.*	*Afterward, I feel depressed when I lose a lot of money.*
I feel the excitement or rush of adrenaline.		
I can be more social.		
It numbs my anxious feelings.		
I do not think about my problems.		
It stops me from feeling bored.		
I get rid of my loneliness.		
I relax when I feel stressed.		
It can solve my money problems.		
Other		
Other		
Other		

The world is like a reverse casino. In a casino, if you gamble long enough, you're certainly going to lose. But in the real world, where the only thing you're gambling is, say, your time or your embarrassment, then the more stuff you do, the more you give luck a chance to find you.
~ Scott Adams

My Gambling Habits

This page will help you to explore your habits related to gambling.

Complete each sentence starter by writing about your own experiences with gambling.

The first time I gambled was...
_____
_____

My gambling problem first started...
_____
_____

The frequency at which I gamble is...
_____
_____

I gamble most at...
_____
_____

I gamble most often when...
_____
_____

Gambling has affected my life by...
_____
_____

When I gamble I typically spend...
_____
_____

The times I have successfully quit are...
_____
_____

I have tried to quit on my own, but I...
_____
_____

Are there Benefits of Gambling?

This page will help you to explore the benefits you feel related to gambling. Complete each sentence starter by writing about your own experiences with gambling.

What do you (did you) get out of gambling?

_____

_____

_____

What part has gambling played in your life?

_____

_____

_____

When do you gamble most often?

_____

_____

_____

How do you feel while gambling?

_____

_____

_____

How do you feel before and after gambling?

_____

_____

_____

How do you feel when not gambling?

_____

_____

_____

What are your dreams/fantasies related to gambling?

_____

_____

_____

Family and Cultural Traditions

All cultures have their own traditions related to gambling. Therefore, the culture in which you grew up will say a lot about your attitudes about gambling. This page will help you to explore your cultural and family traditions related to gambling. Complete each sentence starter by writing about your own experiences with gambling.

How was your first gambling experience related to your culture?

Describe any gambling in your family when you were growing up.

What were your family attitudes toward gambling?

What role did gambling play in family activities and traditions?

What forms of gambling were popular in your culture?

Describe the members of your family who gambled.

What was your culture's view of gambling?

My Strengths and Skills

Everyone has certain strengths they can rely on when dealing with their gambling issues.

Think about your strengths. In the hexagons below, identify the strengths and skills that you have used to cope with gambling problems. Place a check mark by those that have worked best for you.

For example, strengths may include your support system, developing a network of non-gambling friends, your willpower, using gardening skills as an alternative activity when bored, etc.

My
Strengths
& Skills

Costs of My Gambling

In addition to finances, gambling is costing you many things in your life.

On the line under each of the ways gambling can take its toll on you, place an X on the continuum. On the dotted line below each one, write why you rated yourself that way. Be honest.

What are the financial or legal costs of your gambling?

0 (Not Much) 5 (A Little) 10 (A Great Deal)

What are the family and relationship costs of your gambling?

0 (Not Much) 5 (A Little) 10 (A Great Deal)

What are the employment/career costs of your gambling?

0 (Not Much) 5 (A Little) 10 (A Great Deal)

What are the physical and medical costs of your gambling?

0 (Not Much) 5 (A Little) 10 (A Great Deal)

What are the emotional costs of your gambling?

0 (Not Much) 5 (A Little) 10 (A Great Deal)

The HIGHER your score on each of the scales above, the more of a gambling problem you have in the specific aspect measured by the assessment. Areas where you scored low suggest that you are not experiencing many signs of a gambling addiction in those areas.

Remember that by selecting even ONE answer, you can be at risk for experiencing devastating effects on your personal and professional lives.

How will these things change if you stop gambling?

0 (Not Much) 5 (A Little) 10 (A Great Deal)

Do you want to stop gambling?

0 (Not Much) 5 (A Little) 10 (A Great Deal)

Factors Affecting Progression

There are many different factors that affect your progression to a gambling addiction.

Write about the following factors that are present in your life:

My Access to Gambling

_____

_____

My Access to Money

_____

_____

My Understanding of Risks

_____

_____

External Factors: You can control your thinking to prevent gambling activities.

Situation(s) that prompt my gambling:

Time(s) I usually gamble:

Place(s):

Substitution activities in which I could engage:

My gambling-related addictive thoughts that verify that I need to gamble and it is okay!

List the thoughts that fuel and perpetuate your gambling.

Example: "I feel lucky today" or "I won't lose when I wear this shirt."

_____

_____

_____

_____

Medical Evaluation

It is important to explore how your health has been impacted by gambling.

Below, describe how you are currently being affected.

My Physical Health

_____

_____

My Emotional Health

_____

_____

Substance Abuse

_____

_____

Side Effects

In addition to the monetary impact of gambling, there are many psychological and physical side effects.

Describe your side effects below.

Anxiety: _____

_____

Depression: _____

_____

Insomnia: _____

_____

Stomach problems: _____

_____

Heart problems: _____

_____

Abuse issues: _____

_____

Suicidal thoughts and attempts: _____

_____

Emotional health: _____

_____

Academic and/or work performance: _____

_____

Eating/food issues: _____

_____

Case Study

Jocelyn is not a very religious person, but she does consider herself spiritual. She takes time to pray each night, and often prays just before gambling. She believes in a higher power, especially when she is winning.

How would you describe Jocelyn's religious approach?

_____

_____

_____

What is your involvement with formal religious groups, practices, and/or beliefs?

_____

_____

_____

How would you describe your relationship with a higher power or philosophy?

_____

_____

_____

Do you believe a higher power can affect whether you win or lose while gambling?

_____

_____

_____

How would you describe your value system?

_____

_____

_____

What gives meaning to your life?

_____

_____

_____

How does gambling add or detract from the meaning in your life?

_____

_____

_____

© 2021 WHOLE PERSON ASSOCIATES, 101 WEST 2ND STREET, SUITE 203, DULUTH MN 55802 • 800-247-6789 • WHOLEPERSON.COM

What Have I Lost?

People often experience financial hardships due to gambling. Some lose their home, car, job, and important personal possessions due to gambling.

Below: write, draw or doodle up to four personal possessions you have lost due to gambling.

I have lost ...	I have lost ...
How I Can Make Amends:	How I Can Make Amends:
I have lost ...	I have lost ...
How I Can Make Amends:	How I Can Make Amends:

Social and Environmental Factors

Living in an environment where gambling is practiced and accepted will increase one's chances of becoming addicted to gambling. People new to retirement, unemployed, or who have a lot of free time may be at risk. People who take care of others may see gambling as an escape or as well-deserved me-time.

Social and environmental factors such as isolation from others, peer pressure to gamble, the frequent use of drugs or alcohol, and easy access to various forms of gambling may contribute to problem gambling.

Below, identify the social and environmental factors that affect your gambling behavior. Describe how you can remedy the social or environmental factors to decrease your chances of gambling.

Social & Environmental Factors	**How I Remedy Them**
Example: Going to bars on the weekends	*Example: Go to a movie or concert.*

_____   _____

_____   _____

_____   _____

_____   _____

On the flip side, there are some social and environmental factors that you can use to decrease your chances of gambling, including support networks, hobbies, and a budget that restricts your access to money to gamble.

Below, identify the social and environmental factors that affect your gambling behavior in a positive way. Describe how you can continue to use them to decrease your chances of gambling.

Social & Environmental Factors	**How I Can Use Them**
Example: Family unit	*Example: Being with my family and spending time them rather than gambling.*

_____   _____

_____   _____

_____   _____

_____   _____

Stressors in My Life

Stress is a part of everyone's life! Whether it is at work, at home, or with friends, you will probably experience stress. Rather than learning and practicing ways of reducing the stress, many people turn to gambling when they are feeling stressed. Stress can be a huge trigger for gambling activities.

Identify two of your primary stressors, ways gambling affects the stress, and better ways to manage the stress.

A stressor in my life:
Ways it pushes me to gamble:
Ways gambling affects the stress:
A better way to manage this stress:
A stressor in my life:
Ways it pushes me to gamble:
Ways gambling affects the stress:
A better way to manage this stress:

Following are some techniques for quickly reducing stress (rather than gambling!)

Deep Breathing: Begin by focusing on a calmer state of mind as you distract yourself from overwhelming thoughts and sensations related to gambling behavior. Sit in a quiet area. Take a slow, deep breath through your nose, allowing both your stomach and chest to rise. Once your stomach is fully expanded, breathe out through your mouth, just as slowly as when you were breathing in. Continue this until your stress is reduced.

Music: When you begin to have the urge to gamble due to stress, music can relax your body and your mind, and take the urge to gamble away. Identify the best type of music that will relax you.

Exercise: With exercise, your body releases endorphins. Endorphins make you feel good. They are like a natural anti-depressant that can counteract the negative feelings produced by the stress. With low to moderate intensity exercise, you can reduce tension, improve sleep, and stabilize your mood. Suggestions for regular exercise activities include brisk walking, jogging, yoga, and going to the gym.

The Gambling Addiction Workbook — **MY GAMBLING HISTORY**

Planning for Change

If you want to change an addiction, you will need to plan for the changes you want to make. In the spaces that follow, identify the ways in which you envision your life to be.

What, specifically, would you like to be different?

_____

_____

_____

What, specifically, could you do to get started?

_____

_____

_____

If the first step is successful, then what?

_____

_____

_____

Who else could you ask for support or assistance?

_____

_____

_____

What could you ask for?

_____

_____

_____

What would be signs that things are going well?

_____

_____

_____

How would you know if you were off-track?

_____

_____

_____

What would you do if you got off-track?

_____

_____

_____

38   © 2021 WHOLE PERSON ASSOCIATES, 101 WEST 2ND STREET, SUITE 203, DULUTH MN 55802 • 800-247-6789 • WHOLEPERSON.COM

Quotes about Gambling

On the lines that follow the quotes, describe what each of these quotes mean to you and how they apply to YOUR life. Which quote speaks to you and your current gambling situation?

As human beings, our greatness lies not so much in being able to remake
the world... as in being able to remake ourselves.
~ Mahatma Gandhi

_____

_____

_____

_____

My recovery must come first so that everything I love in life doesn't have to come last.
~ Anonymous

_____

_____

_____

_____

Nobody stays recovered unless the life they have created is more
rewarding and satisfying than the one they left behind.
~ Anne Fletcher

_____

_____

_____

_____

You cannot solve a problem from the same consciousness that created it.
You must learn to see the world anew.
~Albert Einstein

_____

_____

_____

_____

Gambling

Awareness of Gambling

Name _____

Date _____

Awareness of Gambling Assessment
Introduction and Directions

Many problem gamblers are not aware that they have a problem. They live in denial and choose not to see how their gambling is affecting themselves and the people in their lives. Awareness is often the starting point of one's recovery.

The following assessment contains 15 statements related to your emotional, physical, and cognitive life. This assessment can help you to gauge your level of awareness of the effect of gambling in your life. Read each of the statements and decide whether or not the statement describes you.

If the statement describes you, circle the number in the YES column next to that item. If the statement does not describe you, circle the number in the NO column next to that item. Do not pay attention to the number; just circle the YES or NO.

In the following example, the circled 1 indicates that the person completing this assessment does not believe that the statement describes them:

	YES	NO
I experience anxiety when I am not gambling	(2)	1

This is not a test. Since there are no right or wrong answers, do not spend too much time thinking about your answers. Be sure to respond to every statement.

(Turn to the next page and begin.)

Awareness of Gambling Assessment

Name _____ Date _____

	YES	NO
I experience anxiety when I am not gambling.	2	1
I feel like my situation is hopeless.	2	1
I get depressed if I cannot gamble.	2	1
I feel guilty after I gamble.	2	1
I am ashamed of myself for not being able to control my gambling.	2	1

I. Emotional – TOTAL = _____

	YES	NO
I keep losing or gaining weight.	2	1
I have trouble falling asleep or sleeping way too much.	2	1
I have lost interest in my usual daily activities.	2	1
I experience headaches and other aches and pains.	2	1
I have heart palpitations and racing heart.	2	1

II. Physical – TOTAL = _____

	YES	NO
I have frequent thoughts about my gambling.	2	1
I relive past gambling experiences in my mind.	2	1
I am constantly planning my next gambling experience.	2	1
I think of new ways to gamble.	2	1
I can't stop thinking about the thrill of winning.	2	1

III. Cognitive – TOTAL = _____

*Go to the next page for scoring assessment
results, profile interpretation, and individual descriptions*

Awareness of Gambling Assessment

Descriptions & Profile Interpretations

The assessment you just completed is designed to measure your awareness of the impact of gambling in your life.

For each of the sections on the previous page, count the scores you circled. Put that total on the line marked TOTAL at the end of each section. Transfer your total to the space below:

I.	**Emotional Total**	=	_____
II.	**Physical Total**	=	_____
III	**Cognitive Total**	=	_____

Assessment Profile Interpretation

Individual Scale Scores	Results	Indications
5 to 6 in any single area	Low	Low scores indicate that you have a limited awareness of the impact of the gambling in your life, or gambling has limited impact in your life in this area.
7 to 8 in any single area	Moderate	Moderate scores indicate that you have some awareness of the impact of the gambling in your life, or gambling has some impact in your life in this area.
9 to 10 in any single area	High	High scores indicate that you have a high awareness of the impact of the gambling in your life, or gambling has a high impact in your life in this area.

Individual Scale Descriptions

Emotional   A person scoring LOW on this assessment tends to be unaware or minimally affected by the various emotions that precede, accompany, and exist after a gambling episode.

Physical   A person scoring LOW on this assessment tends to be unaware or minimally affected by the of the various physical changes that are coinciding with their gambling behavior.

Cognitive   A person scoring LOW on this assessment tends to be unaware or minimally affected by the how their thinking can actually trigger a gambling episode.

My Feelings

Even though they often don't realize it at the time, people who are addicted to gambling experience a wide range of emotions.

Fill in the table below. Dig deep to bring back the emotions you feel.

My Feelings	When I Have Them	The Ways I Deal With Them
Example: Restless	*When I tried to cut down on my gambling activities*	*I started a hobby of coin collecting and really got into it!*
Example: Restless	*When I tried to cut down on my gambling activities.*	*I couldn't do it and went right back to gambling in three days.*
AGITATION		
ANXIETY		
BOREDOM		
DEPRESSION		
EMPTINESS		
FRUSTRATION		
GUILT		
INSIGNIFICANCE		
RESTLESS		
THRILL-SEEKING		
OTHER		

Coping Strategy Suggestions That Might Be Useful

Attend a support group	Draw	Listen to music	Take deep breaths
Cheer someone up	Exercise	Practice mindfulness	Talk with a trusted friend
Describe feelings	Go for a walk	Recall your losses	Talk yourself out of it
Donate to help others	Go to a quiet area	Squeeze a stress ball	Write about your issues

Reducing Stress

A person who gambles is often tempted to gamble even more when experiencing stress. Therefore, stress can greatly influence how one manages emotions and the ways it can be a major contributing factor in recovering (or not) from a gambling problem. To reduce stress, it is vital to find new, healthy ways to cope, whether it is physical exercise, meditation, or talking to a trusted person, etc.

Below, write some of the ways you have successfully dealt with stress
as well as some of the ways you have unsuccessfully dealt with stress in your life.

Ways I Have Been Successful
In Managing My Stress

Ways I Have Been Unsuccessful
in Managing My Stress

_____

_____

_____

_____

_____

_____

_____

_____

Talk with other trusted people and compare ways you have successfully managed stress.

Realizing I Have a Problem

The biggest step to overcoming a gambling addiction is to realize that you have a problem. It takes tremendous strength and courage to own up to this, especially if you have lost a lot of money and strained or broken relationships along the way. Do not give up and do not try to go it alone. Many others have been in your shoes and have been able to break the habit and rebuild their lives. You can, too.

Complete the following sentence starters that will help you realize how your gambling addiction affects you and those people in your life.

Example: I realize I have a problem because my family is fed up with me.

I realize I have a problem because...

I realize I have a problem because...

I realize I have a problem because...

I realize I have a problem because...

I realize I have a problem because...

© 2021 WHOLE PERSON ASSOCIATES, 101 WEST 2ND STREET, SUITE 203, DULUTH MN 55802 • 800-247-6789 • WHOLEPERSON.COM

Be Aware!

Casinos, bookies, and online gaming sites will do everything in their power to keep you addicted and coming back and back and back! The rewards "game" goes something like this and it can vary from site to site:

- They provide you with "rewards" cards to use with machines.
- The more you play, the more "points" you receive.
- The points can be redeemed for free meals, shopping, hotel rooms, etc.
- The more points you earn, the MORE ADDICTED YOU BECOME!

Below, explore some of the rewards that have helped to keep you addicted:

Rewards I Receive	Where & What Am I Gambling?	Ways I Can Break Free of the Rewards
Example: Free play every time I bet 20 times.	*Online gambling site for gambling on football scores.*	*Block sports gambling sites on my computer and agree not to access them anymore on any technology.*

With whom in your support system can you discuss this issue and ask for help to fight these temptations?

_____

_____

_____

_____

Destructive Habitual Patterns

It is vital to be aware of the destructive behavioral patterns that drive your gambling. What patterns present themselves with your gambling behaviors? Do you tend to gamble on the same days, same times, same places? Do you gamble after you have had a bad day at work?

In the spaces below, explore your destructive habitual patterns of gambling.

My Gambling Patterns	My Behaviors	How I Can Change the Pattern
Example: *Time of Day*	*I can't fall asleep so I gamble online at about 2 am.*	*Find better sleep habits. I won't watch so much television or drink caffeine before going to sleep.*
Time of Day		
Places		
Certain Days		
Certain People		
Stressful Times		
Sad Times		
Seasons		
Weather		
Other		

© 2021 WHOLE PERSON ASSOCIATES, 101 WEST 2ND STREET, SUITE 203, DULUTH MN 55802 • 800-247-6789 • WHOLEPERSON.COM

Gambling Triggers

One of the most critical aspects of overcoming a gambling addiction is to identify your gambling triggers, and drag them out of your subconscious into your daily awareness.
Doing this drains them of their power to sabotage you.

Complete the following sentence starters as to what triggers your needs to gamble.

My friends' actions trigger my gambling by... _____

_____

_____

My family members trigger my gambling by... _____

_____

_____

The stressors that trigger my gambling include... _____

_____

_____

The gambling options that trigger my gambling include... _____

_____

_____

I say "just one more time" when I... _____

_____

_____

The substances (cigarettes, alcohol, drugs, food, etc.) that trigger my gambling include... _____

_____

_____

Other things that trigger my gambling are... _____

_____

_____

Gambling Emotions—Causes and Effects

It is important to become more aware of your emotions when you are about to gamble and be able to distinguish between their differences. There is always a thought that precedes an emotion as well as a behavior that follows.

Use the table below to identify the cause and effects of your emotions.

An Emotion I Felt	The Thinking that Prompted the Emotion	The Behavior that Followed the Emotion
Example: Irritability	*I was so close to winning big the last time I gambled.*	*Going online to find a game of chance.*
Anger		
Excitement		
Fear		
Irritability		
Loneliness		
Motivation		
Sadness		
Tension		
Other		

What emotional patterns do you notice?

_____

_____

© 2021 WHOLE PERSON ASSOCIATES, 101 WEST 2ND STREET, SUITE 203, DULUTH MN 55802 • 800-247-6789 • WHOLEPERSON.COM

Relieving Unpleasant or Manic Feelings

Gambling addiction is usually an unhealthy coping mechanism for escaping from troubles and discomfort. When problem gamblers experience stress, frustration, excitement, anticipation, disappointment, anger, fear, motivation, or boredom, they often turn to gambling to help ease their pain or restore their emotional balance. It is important to learn to relieve feelings in healthy ways.

Below, write about the feelings you are experiencing when you feel the need to gamble.

Examples: to unwind, I feel lucky, I'm bored or I need money.

There are more effective ways of getting around these feelings rather than gambling!

Comment on the suggestions below each bullet point.

■ **Exercise. What type of exercises do you like to do?**

_____

_____

■ **Spend time with friends who don't gamble. Who are these friends?**

_____

_____

■ **Try a new hobby. What is a new hobby you would consider pursuing?**

_____

_____

■ **Practicing relaxation techniques. What can you do to relax when an urge to gamble strikes?**

_____

_____

■ **Be mindful. Mindfulness is concentrating your attention on what is occurring in the present moment. Mindfulness draws your attention away from a future event that appears anxiety-producing, and focuses it on what you are doing in the present. In mindfulness, you simply quiet your mind, be aware of what is occurring in your body, and observe what is occurring around you. How can you be more mindful?**

_____

_____

Unrealistic Cognitions

Before one experiences the need to gamble, there are unrealistic thoughts that pass through one's head. These thoughts prompt gambling. However, it is possible to turn this unrealistic thinking into more realistic thinking. It is so important to be mindful of what is happening in your own mind as you experience emotions that trigger gambling. When you are paying attention to the unrealistic thoughts that go through your head, you can temper your intense emotions.

Examples:
- *Unrealistic thought in my head: "I'm due to hit it big."*
- *Feelings that follow: The urge to gamble*
- *Where is the evidence? There is no evidence. "People may never be due to hit it big."*
- *More realistic thinking: Keep telling yourself positive thoughts:*
  - *"The odds are I am not going to win" or*
  - *"I don't have the money to gamble....I'll walk my dog instead."*

Now you try. Take two of your usual unrealistic thoughts and work through the process to make your thinking more realistic.

- **Unrealistic thought in my head:**

- **Feelings that follow:**

- **Where is the evidence?**

- **More realistic thinking:**

- **Unrealistic thought in my head:**

- **Feelings that follow:**

- **Where is the evidence?**

- **More realistic thinking:**

LYING

People with an addiction to gambling often lie to cover up their addiction. They are not even aware of how often they lie to others to maintain their addiction. They use lying as a tool to cover their gambling activities. Think about some of the ways that you have told lies to cover up your gambling habits.

Below, identify the people to whom you lie, how you lie, and the consequences of your behavior. Be honest! No one else needs to see this if you choose. It can be for you only.

People To Whom I Lie (Use Name Codes)	How I Do It	Consequences of My Behavior
Example: MBF	She called and said, "Let's go to the movies." I said, "I need to stay home and get some work done." I went to the Casino for three hours.	She came over to the house to help me and was shocked that I wasn't at home. She felt betrayed. We are no longer friends.

The trouble with lying and deceiving is that their efficiency depends entirely
upon a clear notion of the truth that the liar and deceiver wishes to hide.
~ Hannah Arendt

Gambling Denial

Many problem gamblers do not even realize that they have a problem. They live in denial and keep chasing their losses in hopes of hitting it big.

On the line under each example of gambling awareness, place an X on the continuum of how much you relate to the statement. On the dotted line below each one, write why you rated yourself that way. Be HONEST!

I am aware of how much I gamble.

0 (Not Much)   5 (A Little)   10 (A Great Deal)

I am aware of who I hurt by gambling.

0 (Not Much)   5 (A Little)   10 (A Great Deal)

I am aware of what and who triggers my gambling.

0 (Not Much)   5 (A Little)   10 (A Great Deal)

I don't care who I hurt by my gambling.

0 (Not Much)   5 (A Little)   10 (A Great Deal)

I sometimes gamble without even knowing I'm doing it.

0 (Not Much)   5 (A Little)   10 (A Great Deal)

I I am aware of the consequences of my gambling.

0 (Not Much)   5 (A Little)   10 (A Great Deal)

I often gamble when I feel good.

0 (Not Much)   5 (A Little)   10 (A Great Deal)

Life's Challenges

Using gambling to cope with life's challenges is one of the biggest predictors of an eventual gambling addiction. These challenges can be positive or negative.

In the spaces below, write about the life challenges that are (or have) triggered your gambling, how you react to the challenges, and how you can resolve these challenges.

My Life Challenges	How I React	How I Can Resolve the Challenge Without Gambling
Example: I just got written up at work.	I gamble because I am feeling scared and gambling makes me feel powerful.	Instead, discuss the issues with my partner and write up a response for my supervisor.

I think that life is difficult. People have challenges. Family members get sick, people get older, you don't always get the job or the promotion that you want. You have conflicts in your life. And really, life is about your resilience and your ability to go through your life and all of the ups gand downs with a positive attitude.
~ Jennifer Hyman

Impulsiveness

There are many impulses that can trigger a desire to gamble. Some of these impulses that can trigger a gambling addiction include decision-making without thinking things through, the need for immediate rewards, and the use and abuse of certain substances like alcohol.

In the circles below, identify the impulses that trigger your desire to gamble.
Next to each, write about how the impulses drive your behavior.

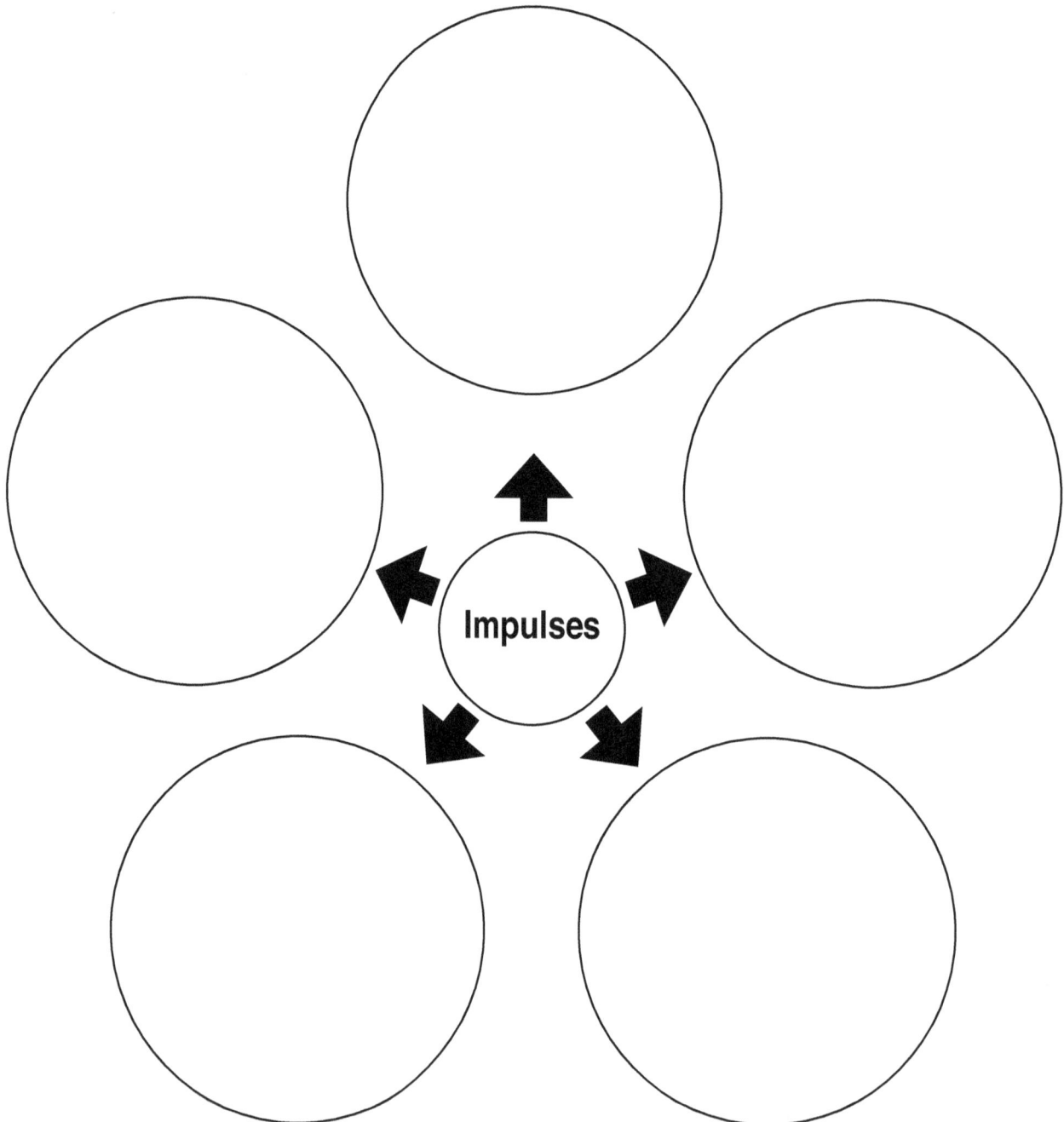

Impulses

Some ways to overcome these impulses include practicing yoga, meditating to reduce your irrational thinking, mindfulness to stay attentive to the task at hand, deep breathing, and other healthy methods that relieve stressful impulses without putting your health and well-being at risk.

© 2021 WHOLE PERSON ASSOCIATES, 101 WEST 2ND STREET, SUITE 203, DULUTH MN 55802 • 800-247-6789 • WHOLEPERSON.COM

Cycle of Problem Gambling

Problem gambling is a predictable cycle. It begins with the loss of large amounts of money. This loss triggers feelings like severe depression, which may lead to suicidal thoughts, self-destructive behavior, or attempted suicide. In order to alleviate feelings of depression and despair, gamblers may use this addictive process as a way to escape or to fix their problems. Gambling thus becomes a cycle in which the elation or depression that follow an episode lead to greater risk-taking and higher bets.

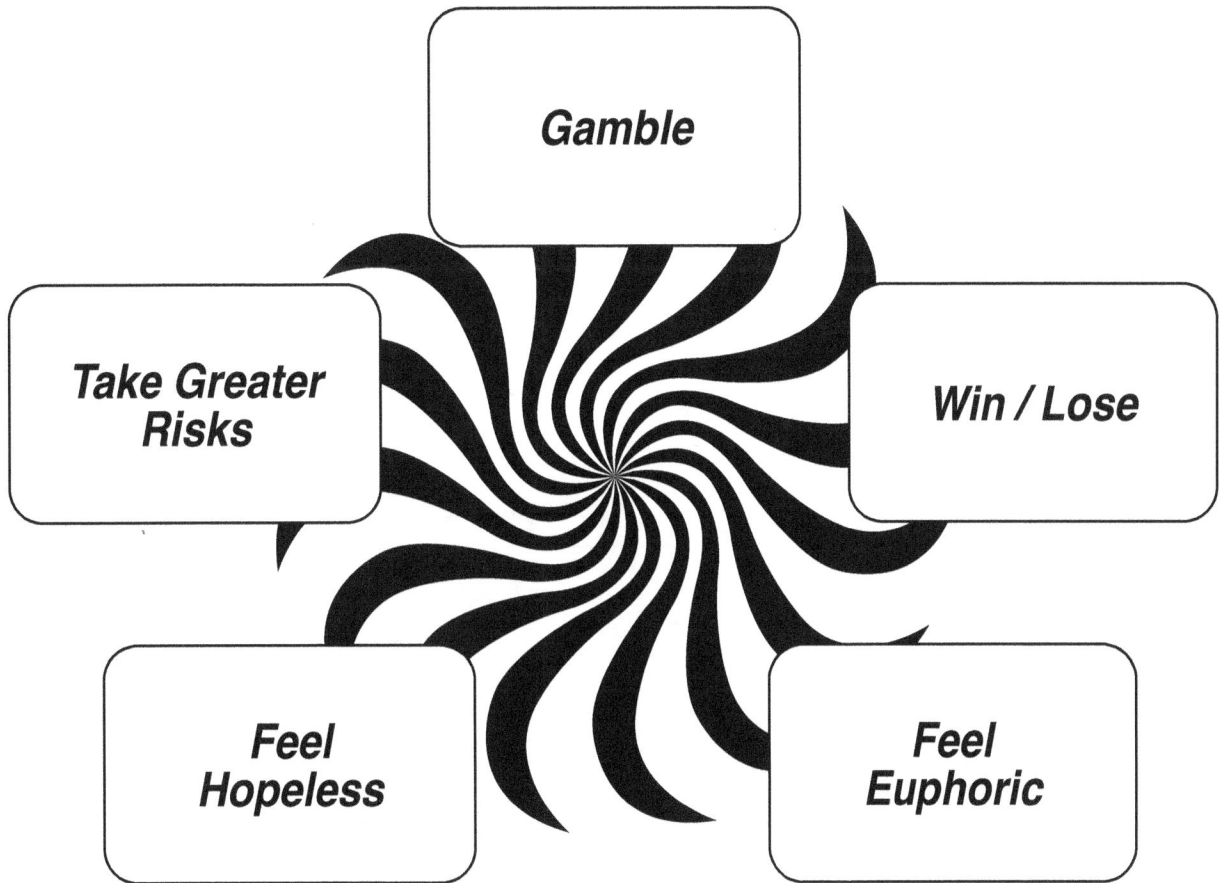

Gamble

Win / Lose

Take Greater Risks

Feel Euphoric

Feel Hopeless

How does this Cycle of Problem Gambling play out in your life?

_____

_____

_____

_____

_____

Reflection of Loss

Problem gamblers have short memories and they easily forget when they lose money.

Below, remember the feeling when you last lost a great deal of money at the casino, online, or through a sports betting establishment. Allow yourself to feel that despondency when you are having thoughts about gambling again. Write a description of that time below:

Where I was gambling:
What I was betting on:
How much I lost:
How I felt afterward:
The consequences of this gambling episode:

Put this page of your mental image somewhere where you can see it every time you get the urge to gamble. Along with this image, try saying these positive affirmations to yourself.

- I will be free of my gambling addiction.
- I can be stronger than my desire to gamble.
- I am a rational and responsible individual and will behave that way.
- I am now changing my life and breaking free from gambling addiction.
- I am now in control of my own impulses.
- I know that I am able to overcome the urge to gamble.
- I will find no thrill in gambling when I remember the consequences.

Lost Trust

It is important to explore the issue of trust in your life. You can do this by journaling about those people whose trust you have lost, what it means to you personally and professionally and what you can do to earn back their trust.

Complete the table that follows to explore trust in your life.

People Whose Trust I Have Lost (USE NAME CODES)	What it Means to Me Personally & Professionally	Ways I Can Earn Back This Person's Trust
Example: My supervisor at work.	*I have lost a few opportunities for a promotion.*	*Work overtime and volunteer for projects that will help my supervisor*

Who is the first person whose trust you will work hard to earn back and why?

Name Code ___ ___ ___

_____

_____

_____

_____

My Support Network

Many people addicted to gambling are not always aware of their supporters. If they are aware of them, they do not reach out to them. It is important to identify and strengthen your support network. It is difficult to battle any addiction without support. You need to reach out to trusted friends, family, and /or a mental health practitioner.

Some Points to Remember

- It is critical that you do not visit casinos or gamble online.
- Reach out to trusted neighbors, family, friends, mental health practitioner, etc.
- Join a sports team, enroll in an education class, or volunteer for a good cause.
- Join a peer support group such as Gamblers Anonymous. A key part of the program is to find a sponsor, a former gambler who has experienced remaining free from addiction and can provide you invaluable guidance and support.

In the spaces that follow, list the people in your support network:

My Supporters (Use name codes)	Relationship To Me	How They Support Me	How I Could Use or Ask for More Support

Quotes about Awareness

*On the lines that follow the quotes, describe which quotes
speak to you and your current gambling situation.*

Whatever we are waiting for - peace of mind, contentment, grace, the inner
awareness of simple abundance - it will surely come to us, but only when
we are ready to receive it with an open and grateful heart.
~ Sarah Ban Breathnach

_____

_____

_____

The ultimate value of life depends upon awareness and the power
of contemplation rather than upon mere survival.
~ Aristotle

_____

_____

_____

Meditation is to be aware of every thought and of every feeling, never
to say it is right or wrong, but just to watch it and move with it.
In that watching, you begin to understand the whole movement of thought
and feeling. And out of this awareness comes silence.
~ Jiddu Krishnamurti

_____

_____

_____

I believe it's strikingly important to remember that when you know better, you
can do better. With higher levels of awareness, you can make smarter choices.
And the more clarity you get as to who you want to become, the quicker
you can start making the choices need[ed] to get you there.
~ Robin S. Sharma

_____

_____

_____

Gambling

Money Issues

Name _____

Date _____

Money Issues Assessment
Introduction and Directions

Many problem gamblers are willing to risk something they value in the hope of getting something of even greater value. Gambling is fraught with problems including people continually chasing bets that lead to greater losses, hiding their spending behavior, depleting their savings, accumulating debt, or even resorting to theft or fraud to finance their addiction.

The following assessment contains 20 statements related to money issues faced by people with a gambling problem. Read each of the statements and decide whether or not the statement describes you.

If the statement describes you, circle the YES column next to that item.
If the statement does not describe you, circle the NO column next to that item.

In the following example, the circled YES indicates that the statement describes the person completing this assessment.

Due to my gambling ...

I always seem to need more money. . . . . (YES) . . . . NO

This is not a test. Since there are no right or wrong answers, do not spend too much time thinking about your answers. Be sure to respond to every statement. BE HONEST!

(Turn to the next page and begin.)

Money Issues Assessment

Name _____ Date _____

Due to my gambling ...

I always need more money.	YES . . . . NO
I keep on applying for new credit cards.	YES . . . . NO
My money just seems to disappear.	YES . . . . NO
I become uncomfortable when people talk about money.	YES . . . . NO
I have hurt some people.	YES . . . . NO
I have lost control over how much I wager when gambling.	YES . . . . NO
I rely on others to provide me with money to gamble.	YES . . . . NO
I am in a terrible financial situation (mortgage, car, credit cards, etc.)	YES . . . . NO
I keep gambling when I am losing until I win.	YES . . . . NO
I feel the need to earn back money I have lost.	YES . . . . NO
When I lose, I am unpleasant at home.	YES . . . . NO
I feel compelled to keep going until I've spent the last dollar.	YES . . . . NO
I often increase my bet amounts when I am losing.	YES . . . . NO
I spend money that I cannot afford to lose.	YES . . . . NO
I use money intended for bills, mortgage, etc.	YES . . . . NO
I have experienced financial hardships.	YES . . . . NO
I have lost important personal possessions.	YES . . . . NO
I have borrowed money illegally.	YES . . . . NO
I have stolen from others.	YES . . . . NO
I have gambling debts.	YES . . . . NO

YES Answers – TOTAL = _____

*Go to the next page for scoring assessment
results, profile interpretation, and individual descriptions*

Money Issues Assessment

Descriptions & Profile Interpretations

The assessment you just completed is designed to measure the impact that gambling is having on your financial life.

Count the number of YES answers you circled on the Money Issues Assessment. Put that total on the line marked TOTAL at the end of the section on the assessment. Transfer your total to this space below:

Money Issues Total   =   _____

~~~~~~

Assessment Profile Interpretation

By circling even ONE YES answer, you are presently at risk for developing or having a gambling addiction. The more YES answers you circled, the greater the risk you have for experiencing a problem with your gambling.

Money Issues Total _____

This assessment measures the impact of gambling on your finances.

Remember that even one "YES" score can suggest you are experiencing gambling addiction money issues.

The HIGHER your score on the Money Issues Assessment, the more of a money issue you have due to your gambling.

Enter your score on the line above, then transfer it to the continuum below.

6 = Low	**10 = Moderate**	**20 = High**

~~~~~~

What is your reaction to your score?

_____

_____

_____

_____

Ways I Get Money

People with a gambling problem are often very resourceful when it comes to securing money to support their gambling habit. They may borrow money from illegal sources, open new checking accounts, apply for additional credit cards, or even steal from others.

Below, identify some of the ways you have managed to get money with which to gamble, how much, and how you will pay it back. BE HONEST! No one else needs to see this paper.

Ways I Get Money	Approximately How Much	How I Will Repay it
I stole it from my friend's wallet	$150.00	After I win, I will pay my friend back.

The most beautiful things are not associated with money; they are memories and moments. If you don't celebrate those, they can pass you by.
~ Alek Wek

What does the above quote mean to you?

_____

_____

_____

How can you begin to make memories and moments rather than gambling?

_____

_____

_____

© 2021 WHOLE PERSON ASSOCIATES, 101 WEST 2ND STREET, SUITE 203, DULUTH MN 55802 • 800-247-6789 • WHOLEPERSON.COM

Things I've Neglected

Addictive gamblers often spend money they do not have for gambling purposes. They may use money for gambling that is needed for important things like rent, the mortgage, car payments, credit card bills, food, utility bills, etc.

What are some of the things you have neglected to pay in order to have more money with which to gamble? Write about them in the hexagon spaces below. BE HONEST!

I've
Neglected

My Money Problems

It is vital to explore the severity of the various money issues you may be dealing with.

Which do you think are the most troublesome money issues for you? For each of the ten items listed below, on the line to the left, rank order each of them from the most troublesome (1) to least troublesome (10). In the line after each item, explain why you ranked it where you did.

_____ **Receiving calls from creditors** _____

_____ **Mounting debt**_____

_____ **Unexplained cash advances on credit cards** _____

_____ **Unexplained assets that have disappeared from the home** _____

_____ **Bank accounts drained**_____

_____ **Sudden, unexpected bills** _____

_____ **New loans taken out**_____

_____ **Money for bills used for gambling** _____

_____ **No money for everyday living for self and/or family**_____

_____ **Threatening bill collectors coming to the door** _____

Now that you have ranked your money issues,
write about how you will deal with the most troublesome issues.

Write about a trusted person that you can talk with, NOT to loan you money,
but to help you straighten this out.

Cut Off My Gambling Dollars page 1

Compulsive gamblers can get the urge to place a bet at any time. It is important to try and create a buffer between the gambler and money. With less access to money, gamblers will have less of a chance to impulsively gamble this money away.

In the box to the left, check off the actions you have tried and write about how successful it was in helping you reduce your access to gambling.

☐ I closed credit accounts that could feed my gambling problem. _____

☐ I got rid of credit cards._____

☐ I got rid of ATM cards. _____

☐ I had my bank require two signatures for a withdrawal, one from me and one from a trusted friend

  or relative. _____

☐ I had a close family member handle my money._____

☐ I kept only a small amount of cash in my wallet so I'm not tempted to spend my money on gambling.

  _____

☐ I asked that my access to household finances be restricted or cut off entirely._____

☐ I needed to go to a trusted family member or friend for money._____

☐ I cut off on-line access to money. _____

☐ I was given an "allowance" to spend._____

☐ I transferred legal control of bank accounts, investments, home and car to trusted individual(s).____

☐ I sought professional financial and tax advice. _____

☐ I sought financial legal advice. _____

☐ I consolidated my debt. _____

☐ Other:_____

(Continued on the next page)

Cut Off My Gambling Dollars page 2

Think about some of the ways (see page 1) to cut off your sources of gambling finances.

*In the boxes below, draw, doodle, or write about four steps you will take
to further ensure that you will cut yourself off from your source of gambling finances.*

Step 1	Step 2

Step 3	Step 4

What I've Sold

Many people who are addicted to gambling resort to selling off their possessions to finance a gambling habit. These possessions might include a business, home, car, furniture, jewelry, family mementoes, etc.

What are some of the most important possessions you have sold or pawned
to finance your gambling addiction?
Draw them in the spaces that follow. BE HONEST!

Things I Have Sold or Pawned

My Payback Plan: Creditors, etc.

A gambling debt is no different than other types of financial debt. It needs to be paid back!

People who gamble often owe multiple creditors money that they cannot afford to lose. It is important to develop a plan to pay back the creditors in your life.

Below, list those whom you owe, how much money you owe, and how you will pay them back.

My Creditors	How Much I Owe	How I Will Pay Back
Example: Bookies	*$500*	*Contact and ask if I can make small, but regular payments every month. I will stop gambling and start putting certain amounts away at every paycheck.*
Bookies		
Casinos		
Loan Sharks		
Credit Cards		
Bank – Personal Loans		
Bank – Home Equity Loans		
Credit Unions		
Retirement Plans		
Life Insurance		
Other		
Other		

My Payback Plan: Individuals

In addition to your creditors, you might have borrowed money from many individuals. These might be partners, spouses, friends, children, parents, and even strangers.

Identify the people from whom you have borrowed money,
how much you have borrowed, and how you will pay them back.

People from Whom I Have Borrowed Money (Use Name Codes)	How Much Money I Borrowed	How I Will Pay Them Back

Following are some tips for paying off creditors and people to whom you owe money:
- The longer you wait, the more interest you rack up through credit accounts.
- Pay off any amount at all, as soon as you can, to show good faith.
- Even if you cannot pay people off immediately, develop a plan with them for repaying the money you owe to them.

Create a Budget Page 1

To get your life back under control you need a spending plan, also known as a budget. This ensures that you will direct the money you earn to where it needs to go (bills, mortgage, loans, food, other necessities, etc.) This plan will help you avoid debt and spend less than you earn. It will also help you to meet your savings goals.

Monthly Income Sources

List only income that can be counted on each month: (paychecks, child support, interest, social security benefits, etc. Income that varies, such as sales commissions and tips should be averaged on a monthly basis.

Extra Income Sources

List year-end bonuses at work, an income-tax refund, freelance income, tips, etc. These generally should be put toward savings or investing goals, or special needs.

© 2021 WHOLE PERSON ASSOCIATES, 101 WEST 2ND STREET, SUITE 203, DULUTH MN 55802 • 800-247-6789 • WHOLEPERSON.COM

Create a Budget Page 2

Below, list your basic monthly household expenses.
Write notes to yourself (comments or reminders) on the line to the right.
If some of the items do not apply to you, write in something applicable to you.

My Monthly Budget

Monthly Expenses	Amount Paid	Notes
Living Expenses		
Mortgage/Rent	$_____	_____
Utilities	$_____	_____
Telephone	$_____	_____
Cable/streaming services	$_____	_____
Internet service	$_____	_____
Taxes	$_____	_____
Household repairs/upkeep	$_____	_____
Transportation Expenses		
Bus/train/taxi fare	$_____	_____
Car payment/rental	$_____	_____
Gasoline	$_____	_____
Parking	$_____	_____
Car repairs	$_____	_____
Entertainment Expenses		
Sporting events	$_____	_____
Movies	$_____	_____
Eating out	$_____	_____
Vacations	$_____	_____
Other entertainment	$_____	_____
Medical expenses		
Medical expenses	$_____	_____
Dental expenses	$_____	_____
Prescriptions	$_____	_____
Insurance		
Life insurance	$_____	_____
Health insurance	$_____	_____
Auto insurance	$_____	_____
Homeowners/Renters insurance	$_____	_____
Food and Clothes		
Food (total grocery expenses)	$_____	_____
Clothes	$_____	_____
Family Expenses		
Child care	$_____	_____
Toys/games/activities	$_____	_____
Child support payments	$_____	_____
School tuition/supplies	$_____	_____
Pet care	$_____	_____
Other Debt		
Credit card interest	$_____	_____
School costs/loans	$_____	_____
Newspaper/Magazine subscriptions	$_____	_____
TOTAL MONTHLY EXPENSES	$_____	_____

Enablers

Compulsive gambling and repeated gambling losses take a tremendous toll not only on the person managing or earning the money, but also on the entire family. Well-meaning family members, often a partner of the gambler, try to help the gambler by lending them money, bailing them out of money issues, paying their bills, and stashing money to gamble.
These are called ENABLERS!

CHARACTERISTICS OF AN ENABLER

- They ignore or make excuses for someone's addictive gambling.
- Their actions encourage empowerment or dependence on them.
- They consistently put their own needs and desires aside in order to help the addicted gambler.
- Their actions are motivated by pity, fear, caring, and guilt.
- They continue to offer help that is often not appreciated nor acknowledged by the addicted gambler.

Who are your enablers? Below, identify those people and how they enable you.

Enablers (Use Name Codes)	How This Person Enables Me to Gamble
Example: MWM	*She keeps saying that I am due to win and slips me some of the grocery money.*
Example: MBF	*He gives me money and tells me to split the profits with him.*

© 2021 WHOLE PERSON ASSOCIATES, 101 WEST 2ND STREET, SUITE 203, DULUTH MN 55802 • 800-247-6789 • WHOLEPERSON.COM

Family Financial Abuse

Problematic gambling can lead to the destructive breakup of relationships. Families often experience divorce, domestic violence, child abuse, and financial abuse.

Describe some of the ways you have financially abused your family members.

Forms of Financial Abuse	Family Member(s) (USE NAME CODES)	How It Affects These Family Members
I withhold money.		
I control how all of the money is spent.		
I do not allow access to bank accounts.		
I refuse or delay child support.		
I hide assets.		
I steal money.		
I steal objects to sell.		
I withhold food money.		
I withhold allowances.		
I neglect to contribute to the family income.		
Other.		
Other.		

Feeding the Habit

People who are addicted to gambling need to realize where the money comes from to feed their gambling habit and how it affects them and other people in their lives.

List sources of income and available assets that are financing this habit.

Obvious sources of income (salary, tips, royalties, etc.) *How does this affect me and the others in my life?*
Less obvious sources of income (bank accounts, cds, mutual funds, stocks and bonds, IRAs, home equity, interests in a small business, real estate, life insurance policies.) *How does or could this affect me and the others in my life?*
People who lend me money. *How does or could this affect me and the others in my life?*
Illegal sources of income (bookies, etc.) *How does or could this affect me and the others in my life?*
Things I have sold or pawned, or will sell or pawn (cars, boat, jewelry, antiques, art, furnishings, a coin collection, appliances, etc.) *How does or could this affect me and the others in my life?*
Other Stashes: *How does or could this affect me and the others in my life?*

Sources of feeding a gambling addiction and its effect on oneself and others need to be recognized and tracked on a regular basis.

Who is a trusted family member or friend who can monitor your finances?

_____

_____

Criminal Activity

Many people with a gambling problem resort to criminal activities in order to finance their gambling habit. This can include robbing people, fraud, blackmail, stealing, selling objects that are not their own, and embezzling money.

Below, identify any criminal activities in which you have been involved in to get money.
Be honest – no one needs to see this - but you do!

Types of Criminal Activity	Who Was Involved (USE NAME CODE)	Caught or Not?
Example: Stealing money from individuals	*I take money from MHJ's wallet.*	*No, not yet*
Example: Stealing money from individuals	*I took money from MHJ's wallet.*	*Yes, and he told me if I ever did that again, I would lose my job.*
Stealing money from individuals		
Stealing objects from people and selling them.		
Robbery		
Fraud		
Blackmail		
Embezzling		
Other		

Money Issues Case Study

James started gambling by playing video poker. He was losing about $250.00 each day. For a while he was able to hide his gambling problem, but eventually his partner found out. His partner tried to help him as much as possible by bailing him out and paying some of the bills. James promised to quit, but he didn't.

Do James and his partner have a problem? Explain.

_____

_____

_____

How would you describe James' situation?

_____

_____

_____

What role is James' partner playing in this case?

_____

_____

_____

What should James do?

_____

_____

_____

What should his partner do?

_____

_____

_____

What advice would you give to James and his partner?

_____

_____

_____

Is this similar to anything in your life? Explain.

_____

_____

_____

Quotes about Money Issues

On the lines that follow each of the quotes,
describe what they mean to you and how they apply to YOUR life.

Money can get rid of your financial problems,
but it won't get rid of your emotional problems.
~ Sonya Parker

_____

_____

_____

It's not how much money you make, but how much money you keep, how hard it
works for you, and how many generations you keep it for.
~ Robert Kiyosaki

_____

_____

_____

Never spend your money before you have earned it.
~ Thomas Jefferson

_____

_____

_____

You can't pay enough money to... cure that feeling of being broken and confused.
~ Winona Ryder

_____

_____

_____

Which quote especially speaks to you and your money issues? Why?

_____

_____

_____

_____

Gambling

Effects of Gambling

Name _____

Date _____

Effects of Gambling Assessment
Introduction and Directions

A gambling addiction can affect many areas of a person's life including family, social, financial, and work. The *Effects of Gambling Assessment* was designed to help you explore the ways gambling affects you as well as others in your life.

This assessment contains 30 statements that are related to various ways gambling can affect your life and the lives of those around you. Read each of the statements and decide whether or not the statement describes you.

If the statement is TRUE, circle the number next to that item under the "True" column.

If the statement is FALSE, circle the number next to that item under the "FALSE" column.

In the example below, the circled number 2 under "TRUE"
indicates the statement is true of the person completing the individual scale about emotions.

	TRUE	FALSE
Due to my gambling …		
I am often moody.	(2)	1

This is not a test. Since there are no right or wrong answers, do not spend too much time thinking about your answers. Be sure to respond to every statement. Be Honest!

(Turn to the next page and begin.)

Effects of Gambling Assessment (Page 1)

Name _____ Date _____

This will only be accurate if you respond honestly.
No one else needs to see this if you choose to keep it private.

EMOTIONAL SCALE_____ **TRUE**   **FALSE**

Due to my gambling ...

I am often moody. 2 1

I feel sad a lot. 2 1

I feel guilty about my gambling. 2 1

I feel embarrassed when talking about my gambling. 2 1

I do not feel good unless I am gambling. 2 1

Emotional Scale – TOTAL = _____

OCCUPATIONAL SCALE_____ **TRUE**   **FALSE**

Due to my gambling ...

I miss work a lot. 2 1

I have noticed a decline in my work performance. 2 1

I do not finish tasks or projects on time. 2 1

I have to borrow gambling money from co-workers. 2 1

I go into work late because I stay up late gambling. 2 1

Occupational Scale – TOTAL = _____

PHYSICAL SCALE_____ **TRUE**   **FALSE**

Due to my gambling ...

I am not eating right. 2 1

I need to go to the doctor a lot. 2 1

I am not taking care of myself. 2 1

I am experiencing physical problems. 2 1

I am afraid I will have a serious medical problem. 2 1

Physical Scale – TOTAL = _____

(Continued on the next page)

Effects of Gambling Assessment (Page 2)

Name _____ Date _____

	YES TRUE	NO FALSE
FAMILY SCALE_____		

Due to my gambling ...

	YES TRUE	NO FALSE
I am not trusted by my family.	2	1
I find myself getting into many arguments with family members.	2	1
I fail to keep promises I make to family members.	2	1
I believe my family has no confidence in me.	2	1
I have failed to meet the expectations of my family.	2	1

Family Scale – TOTAL = _____

	TRUE	FALSE
SOCIAL SCALE_____		

Due to my gambling ...

	TRUE	FALSE
I have embarrassed my friends by my behavior.	2	1
I have stolen from my friends.	2	1
I have lost the trust of my friends.	2	1
I have failed to keep promises made to my friends.	2	1
I have lost friends because of my gambling.	2	1

Social Scale – TOTAL = _____

	TRUE	FALSE
RECREATIONAL SCALE_____		

Due to my gambling ...

	TRUE	FALSE
I have not taken part in different fun activities for a long time other than gambling.	2	1
My leisure activities revolve around gambling.	2	1
I usually say no to anyone that asks me to do something, unless it is gambling.	2	1
I don't have an alternative activity to replace gambling.	2	1
I have too much time on my hands.	2	1

Recreational Scale – TOTAL = _____

*Go to the next page for scoring assessment
results, profile interpretation, and individual descriptions*

Effects of Gambling Assessment

Scoring Directions & Profile Interpretations

The assessment you just completed looks at the effects of gambling on various aspects of your life.

On the previous pages, total the scores you circled and put that total in the box marked TOTAL. Then transfer that number below. Place each number on the continuum line of the matching Scale below:

Emotional _____ (This scale measures the extent to which your gambling has affected you emotionally.)

5 = Low	8 = Moderate	10 = High

Occupational _____ (This scale measures the extent to which your gambling has affected you occupationally.)

5 = Low	8 = Moderate	10 = High

Physical _____ (This scale measures the extent to which your gambling has affected you physically.)

5 = Low	8 = Moderate	10 = High

Family _____ (This scale measures the extent to which your gambling has affected your family.)

5 = Low	8 = Moderate	10 = High

Social _____ (This scale measures the extent to which your gambling has affected you socially.)

5 = Low	8 = Moderate	10 = High

Recreational _____ (This scale measures the extent to which your gambling has affected you recreationally.)

5 = Low	8 = Moderate	10 = High

The higher your score in any of the scales, the greater risk you have for experiencing negative effects of gambling. However, by circling even ONE Moderate or High answer, you can be at risk for experiencing devastating effects on your personal and professional lives.

© 2021 WHOLE PERSON ASSOCIATES, 101 WEST 2ND STREET, SUITE 203, DULUTH MN 55802 • 800-247-6789 • WHOLEPERSON.COM

Occupational Functioning

A gambling addiction can cause a lack of functioning in all areas of one's life. Often, people lose their jobs as a result of a gambling problem. This compounds the financial devastation already experienced from the addiction itself.

Below, place a check mark in front of the warning signs that describe you.
In the space by each warning sign you have checked, explain how it pertains to you.

Work-Related Warning Signs Due to Gambling:

☐ **Lost a job** _____

☐ **Decreased productivity** _____

☐ **Made excuses for missing work** _____

☐ **Late to work** _____

☐ **Gambled at work** _____

☐ **In trouble with supervisors** _____

☐ **Failed to finish projects** _____

☐ **Borrowed money from co-workers** _____

☐ **Used phone for gambling-related issues at work** _____

☐ **Talked about gambling problems at work** _____

☐ **Used computer for gambling** _____

☐ **Stole supplies or money from work or co-workers** _____

Learn to enjoy every minute of your life. Be happy now. Don't wait
for something outside of yourself to make you happy in the future.
Think how really precious is the time you have to spend, whether it's at
work or with your family. Every minute should be enjoyed and savored.
~ Earl Nightingale

What ways can your work possibly meet the same needs that are met with your gambling habits?

(Example: create a new project, learn a new skill, take on an additional responsibility, network with co-workers, go above and beyond to get a promotion, etc.)

_____

_____

_____

Legal Problems

People who have a gambling problem often do something illegal to pay for their gambling habit.

If this is true of you, explore your legal problem below.
(Example: arrests for theft, prostitution, breaking and entering, embezzlement, selling stolen goods, etc.)

Be honest! No one needs to see this but you, if you choose to keep it private.

My Legal Problem:

What occurred:

Affect the criminal charges had on my life: *(Ex: custody, restitution, fines, embarrassment, etc.)*

We often learn more from the mistakes we have made than from our accomplishments. What did you learn?

Financial Problems

All people face financial problems at some point in their lives. However, for many problem gamblers, the financial losses become extremely great. Their home may be forced into foreclosure. When bills can't be paid the family may have to declare bankruptcy. Financial problems can include debt, poverty, selling possessions, or borrowing money from anyone at all.

In the circles that follow, identify some of your financial problems.

Be honest! No one needs to see this if you choose to keep it private.

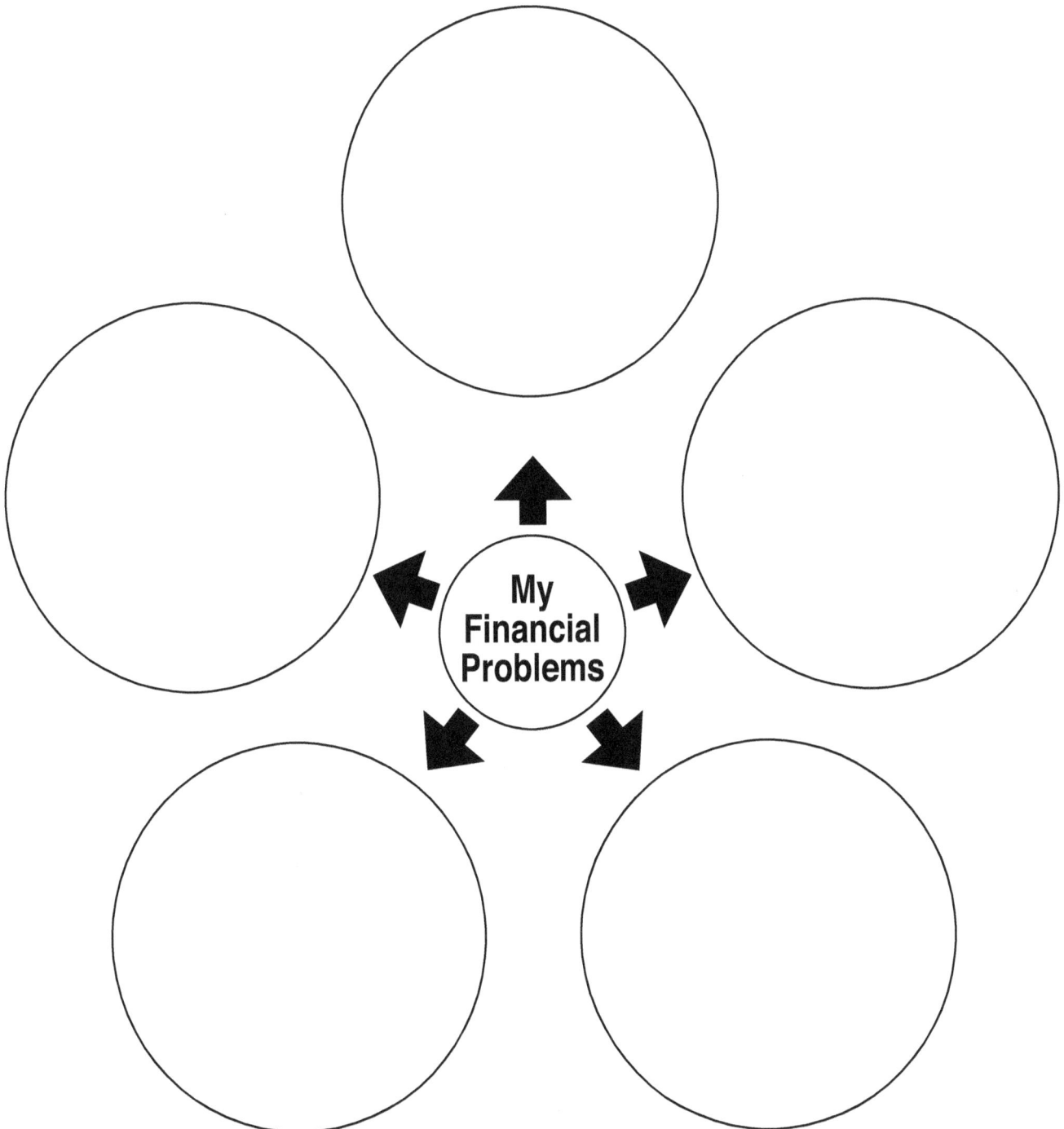

My Financial Problems

Emotional Problems

If you are addicted to gambling, you have probably experienced a wide variety of negative emotions. You need to think about how your gambling negatively impacts your emotional and mental health. Because of these emotions, you may have trouble making it through the day until you gamble next.

Identify when you tend to experience the emotions listed and how you usually cope with them.

Emotions	When I Have These Emotions	How I Usually Cope with Them
Anger		
Anxiety		
Defensiveness		
Embarrassment		
Fear		
Guilt		
Irritability		
Moodiness		
Other		

Try these helpful ways to cope with your emotions:
- Change the thoughts that trigger unwanted emotions to thoughts that prompt positive actions.
- Communicate with others in an assertive way.
- Find creative, healthy ways to lift your mood.
- Find healthy ways to let off steam or effectively express your feelings.
- Remind yourself that gambling is a false fix for emotional issues.
- Talk with a trusted person or counselor about your emotional issues.
- Try to determine what sets your emotions off and avoid responding this way.

Spiritual Well-Being

Your gambling has possibly affected the spiritual side of your nature. Spiritual well-being has the power and capability to provide you with hope, develop meaning and purpose, ground you during periods of instability, give you resiliency to survive, and supply inner peace in the face of adversity. Having a spiritual element in your life can help to heal your gambling addiction.

For each item below, underline if the statement is true or false for you, and explain why.

REGARDING MY GAMBLING

I am unable to find peace. .... TRUE   FALSE

Why?_____

I am irritable until I find my next gambling opportunity. .... TRUE   FALSE

Why?_____

I am unable to find comfort. .... TRUE   FALSE

Why?_____

I feel like I have no purpose in my life other than gambling. .... TRUE   FALSE

Why?_____

I have limited or no hope that everything will be okay. .... TRUE   FALSE

Why?_____

I do not feel supported by almost anyone in my life. .... TRUE   FALSE

Why?_____

I do not feel connected to a higher or spiritual power. .... TRUE   FALSE

Why?_____

Who are some a trusted people with whom you can talk about these feelings?

_____

_____

_____

Recreational Functioning

Gambling can have a significant negative impact on your recreational activities. Because a great deal of your spare-time activities might involve gambling, you have probably limited your involvement in recreational activities.

Below, identify four recreational activities or hobbies in which you have lost interest, but might want to consider revisiting in the future. You can write about them, draw, or doodle pictures of them.

1.	2.
3.	4.

What three steps will you take to begin pursuing one of these activities?

1. _____

_____

2. _____

_____

3. _____

_____

Family Problems

Trying to deal with the stress and tension brought on as a result of a family member's gambling issues can jeopardize the bond among family members. When one's spouse, children, siblings, parents, and other family members can no longer trust a family member, they may feel no sense of security when that person is around, let alone when they are not present, have no confidence in that person, and might even fear the future. The result is a breakdown in the family relationships.

Below, identify some of the ways
you might have jeopardized the bond with your family members.

Ways I Have Jeopardized Bonds with Family Members	Family Members & My Lies (USE NAME CODES)	Ways I Will Attempt to Reconnect & Reassure
Example: Lying	*MHB - I lie to him and tell him that I am working late.*	*Spend less time gambling, more time with him, and be honest.*
Argue, fight, and/or conflicts		
Avoidance		
Being physically, emotionally, verbally, or financially abusive		
Breaking promises		
Hiding things and information from them		
Lying		
Manipulating		
Staying out late or not coming home at all.		
Stealing		
Threatening		
Other		

Psychological Problems

An addiction to gambling is a psychological problem. Aside from liking the thrill of gambling or the chance of winning a lot of money, it can be driven by sadness, anxiety, an inability to control impulses or many other issues. If you are experiencing any of these and they are left untreated, these psychological problems can lead to a sense of despair.

Below, in each section or next to them, identify how you are experiencing the three issues.

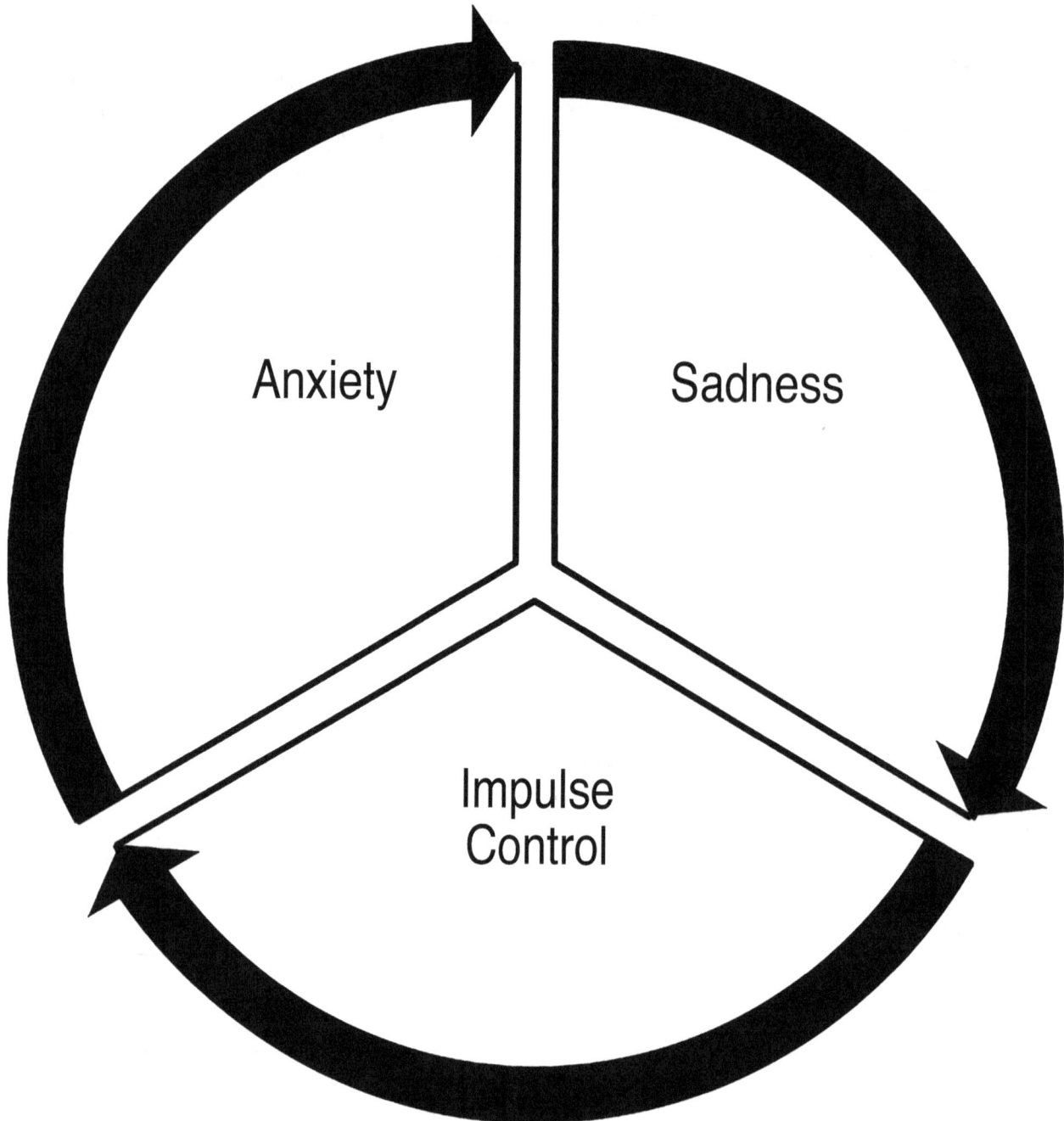

Anxiety

Sadness

Impulse Control

If any of the three of these psychological issues are interfering with your everyday life, you need to see a medical or counseling professional. If you don't have someone, ask a trusted friend to help you find one with whom you connect.

My Friends

Your gambling has probably impacted your relationships with your friends. People with a gambling addiction often get angry with their friends who try and help them, fail to keep promises, steal money from them, and do things so that they lose trust.

Who are four non-gambling friends that you have hurt or lost, and how will you make amends to them?

My Friend (USE NAME CODES)	Ways I Hurt this Person or Lost Our Friendship	Ways I Will Make Amends
Example: KSL	I kept making plans, then failing to follow through.	I will explain what was going on, apologize, make a plan that includes KSL and keep it!

Love is friendship that has caught fire. It is quiet understanding, mutual confidence, sharing and forgiving. It is loyalty through good and bad times. It settles for less than perfection and makes allowances for human weaknesses.

~ Ann Landers

Describe how your good friends have been loyal through good times and through bad times. Use name codes.

_____

_____

_____

Are your gambling friends real friends? Will they continue to be your friends if you stop gambling?

_____

_____

_____

My Physical Health

Usually, anyone struggling with an addiction to gambling has noticed that their health may be deteriorating. It might be from not eating healthy foods and liquids, not getting enough sleep, exercising, visiting a doctor, or taking care of their teeth. These physical problems can truly take a serious toll on health and the neglect of the body can result in very serious consequences.

Below, identify the ways you are neglecting your health,
and how you can start to take better care of yourself.

Ways I am Neglecting My Health	Why I am Neglecting My Health	How I Can Do a Better Job Taking Care of My Health
Example: I am eating all fast foods and my cholesterol is high and my stomach is not happy!	*It is easier to pick up fast food than to cook. Cooking takes time away from gambling!*	*Stay home more and plan and cook meals. Talk to a physician and take medication if needed.*

All the money in the world can't buy you back good health.
~ Reba McEntire

Dependency on Substances

People with a gambling addiction are at risk for drug or alcohol abuse. Some serious gamblers have more than one dependency. This may be an addiction to alcohol, illicit drugs, pharmaceutical drugs used for nonmedical purposes, nicotine, or other types of substances. They may use substances when they are gambling or to help themselves feel okay when not gambling.

What types of substances are you dependent on based on your addiction to gambling?
Be honest! No one needs to see this page if you choose not to show it to anyone.

Type of Substances	How Much and How Often I Use This Substance	The Effects of My Use on Me and on My Relationships
Nicotine		
Alcohol		
Illegal Drugs		
Over-the-Counter Medicine		
Prescription Drugs		
Other		

On what substance are you most dependent?

_____

_____

_____

How can you decrease your dependence?

_____

_____

_____

My Life is Not Hopeless!

Some gamblers feel like their life is hopeless. They feel that they cannot stop gambling and cannot stop hurting other people they care about. They feel they have done things in the past to support their habit that they are ashamed of.

Draw an image of how you see your life right now.	Draw an image of how you want your life to be.

How can you begin to make your image on the right come true?

- It is usually difficult to become motivated, but it may be even more difficult to remain motivated.
- You can do it!
- Goal setting can help enhance your motivation in many different ways including:
  - Visualize your goals with as much clarity as possible.
  - Engage in activities that move you toward your goal.
  - Overcome obstacles that present themselves.
- Persist and never give up!

Hurting Myself

Gambling and the effects of gambling on you and the people you love can cause sadness and anger. As these feelings intensify, you may be tempted to hurt yourself by slashing, burning, or skin carving.

Think about how you have hurt yourself or thought about hurting yourself due to your gambling addiction. Below, list those times, what you did, and how you could have better dealt with your pain.

Ways I Have Hurt Myself or Thought About It	The Effect of My Actions	Alternatives I Could Use
Example: I cut myself.	It didn't help my situation and now I have horrible scars. My family is afraid to say anything to me that might upset me. They nag about my seeking help.	I need to find someone whom I trust to talk with when I am feeling desperate. If that person doesn't work out, I will need to keep looking for someone I connect with.
My Suicidal Thoughts and/or Attempts	**The Effect of My Actions**	**Alternatives I Could Use**
Example: I tried to die by suicide but I got so scared that I stopped.	I left a note to my partner saying what I was going to do. She was so horrified that I might actually succeed at some point that she broke up with me.	Obviously, I need counseling but it's hard to connect with those I've tried. I guess I must keep trying.

Ways to COPE:
- Talk to a medical professional.
- Stick with it until you find someone with whom you can talk.
- Join a Gamblers Anonymous group.
- Get treatment for your gambling addiction.
- Call the National Suicide Prevention Lifeline in the U.S. at 1-800-273-8255 or visit Befrienders Worldwide to find a suicide helpline in your country.

Family Violence Case Study

JYH was gambling more and more and losing more and more money. JYH kept chasing after losses thinking that soon luck would change. Tensions began to escalate with JYH's partner at a dangerous pace. JYH's partner felt like JYH needed to stop gambling and JYH felt cornered. JYH's emotional outbursts ended in violence.

Was JYH justified in the behavior exhibited? Why or why not?

_____

_____

_____

What would you have done if your partner did not approve of your gambling habits?

_____

_____

_____

Have you ever felt cornered about your gambling habits? What did you do?

_____

_____

_____

Do you find yourself getting into arguments and fights at home with family members?

_____

_____

_____

Is it true that the longer out-of-control gambling continues, the greater the potential for bodily harm to family members?

_____

_____

_____

What alternatives did JYH have in this case study?

_____

_____

_____

Quotes about the Effects of Gambling

On the lines that follow each of the quotations,
describe what the quotation means to you and how it applies to YOUR life.

We are all born with a unique genetic blueprint, which lays out the basic
characteristics of our personality as well as our physical health and appearance...
And yet, we all know that life experiences do change us.
~ Joan D. Vinge

_____

_____

_____

Life is about growth and exploration, not achieving a fixed state of balance. You have a
very limited time on earth to experience all that you can. Figuring out how to squeeze
the most out of your family, work, and spirituality is your life's purpose. Go do it.
~ Mel Robbins

_____

_____

_____

The memories we make with our family is [sic] everything.
~ Candace Cameron Bure

_____

_____

_____

Which quote especially speaks to you and the effects of gambling? Why?

_____

_____

_____

_____

_____

Gambling

Finding Healthy Alternatives

Name _____

Date _____

Finding Healthy Alternatives Assessment
Introduction and Directions

For many people who have gambling issues, the ability to quit gambling is largely based on their ability to identify and engage in healthy alternatives to gambling. Gambling is far more accessible than it was in the past. By engaging in healthy leisure-time activities, people can occupy their time and not be tempted to gamble. Leisure interests are those interests that you have in your free time. It is important for you to identify healthy alternatives to gambling. The following assessment can help you get started.

Read each statement carefully. Place a check mark in the boxes of the activities you have enjoyed in the past, or think you might enjoy. See the example below:

In my spare time, I enjoy...

☐ Attending art classes	☑ Planning family recreational activities
☑ Drawing, painting, or sculpting	☐ Cooking and baking
☐ Creating pictures, poems, or stories	☑ Having friends over for dinner
☑ Engaging in arts and crafts	☑ Spending evenings at home with my family
☐ Attending plays or musicals	☑ Taking care of my family
☐ Sewing and needlecrafts	☑ Vacationing with my family
Arts & Crafts = _____	**Home & Family = _____**

In the above example, the person completing the assessment is interested in: two of the activities listed under Arts & Crafts, and five of the activities listed under Home & Family.

This is not a test. Since there are no right or wrong answers, do not spend too much time thinking about your answers. Be sure to respond to every statement.

(Go to the next page to begin the actual assessment.)

Finding Healthy Alternatives Assessment

Name _____ Date _____

In my spare time, I enjoy...

☐ Attending art classes
☐ Drawing, painting, or sculpting
☐ Creating pictures, poems, or stories
☐ Engaging in arts and crafts
☐ Attending plays or musicals
☐ Sewing and needlecrafts

Arts & Crafts = _____

☐ Planning family recreational activities
☐ Cooking and baking
☐ Having friends over for dinner
☐ Spending evenings at home with my family
☐ Taking care of my family
☐ Vacationing with my family

Home & Family = _____

☐ Going to the gym
☐ Walking to get or stay in shape
☐ Attending fitness and nutrition workshops
☐ Taking aerobics and fitness classes
☐ Weightlifting and/or martial arts
☐ Playing sports

Health & Fitness = _____

☐ Repairing computers
☐ Using social media
☐ Playing non-gambling video games
☐ Writing computer programs/software
☐ Creating websites
☐ Troubleshooting technology

Technology = _____

☐ Reading science books and magazines
☐ Visiting museums and/or historical sites
☐ Working mathematical puzzles
☐ Learning about astronomy
☐ Watching the weather
☐ Engaging in scientific research

Science = _____

☐ Using tools
☐ Repairing anything
☐ Working on cars
☐ Creating with wood
☐ Building things
☐ Learning about mechanical principles

Mechanical = _____

☐ Doing volunteer work
☐ Listening to friends with personal problems
☐ Teaching others
☐ Working with children
☐ Helping people with disabilities
☐ Tutoring others

Social = _____

☐ Playing with animals
☐ Raising plants and flowers
☐ Landscaping
☐ Cutting grass and caring for lawns
☐ Having animal pets
☐ Planting and harvesting crops

Plants & Animals = _____

Go to the next page for scoring assessment results, profile interpretation, and individual descriptions

Finding Healthy Alternatives Assessment

Scoring Directions

The assessment you completed will help you identify various types of leisure activities that can help you reduce stress, enhance life satisfaction, and be healthy alternatives to gambling. The assessment is designed to measure your leisure interests and identify activities related to those interests.

Count the number of activities you checked off on the assessment page. Put those totals on the line marked Total at the end of each section. Transfer the totals to the spaces below:

Arts & Crafts	_____	**Home & Family**	_____
Health & Fitness	_____	**Technology**	_____
Science	_____	**Mechanical**	_____
Social	_____	**Plants & Animals**	_____

Profile Interpretation

If you checked 0-2 items in a section, you tend to have limited interest in those types of activities.

If you checked 3-4 items in a section, you tend to have moderate interest in those types of activities.

If you checked 5-6 items in a section, you tend to have high interest in those types of activities.

Activity Descriptions

Below, and on the next page, refer to the scale descriptions in which you scored the highest and circle the leisure activities that can be alternatives to gambling.

1. **Arts & Crafts**
   People scoring high on this scale are interested in expressing themselves creatively through artistic endeavors. Find a way to express your feelings and ideas. Consider such leisure activities as painting, drawing, sketching, sculpting, photography, writing poems, short stories, or music. Try ceramics, pottery, mosaics, origami, reading. Attend arts festivals, try out for a part in community theatre or a local choir. Blog, scrapbook, design web pages, or take dance lessons. Check out the multitude of crafts: quilting, embroidery, weaving, rope-making, canvas work, hooked-rug making, leatherwork, floral design, beadwork, basket weaving, paper making, calligraphy, carpentry, stone carving, jewelry making, etc.

2. **Health & Fitness**
   People scoring high on this scale are interested in physical activities. This is a perfect way to reduce stress and anxiety. Consider such leisure activities as tennis, darts, martial arts, chopping wood, yoga, mountain climbing, kayaking, scuba diving, coaching, amateur sports, weight lifting, health clubs, exercising, jogging, aerobics, softball, skiing, bowling, swimming, traveling, cycling, mall walking, outdoor hiking, canoeing, etc.

(Continued on the next page)

Activity Descriptions (Continued)

3. Science

People scoring high on this scale are interested in discovering, collecting, and analyzing information about the natural world, life sciences, and human behavior. Consider such leisure activities as astronomy, science fairs, healthcare volunteer, building model rockets, mathematical puzzles, amateur archeology, meteorology, star-gazing, collecting rocks, exploring caves, weather watching, visiting planetariums and science museums, studying anatomy, prospecting, doing chemistry experiments, watching aerospace shows on television, etc.

4. Social

People scoring high on this scale are interested in social, mental, emotional, and spiritual well-being. They like to help others. Consider volunteering your time by tutoring, assisting the disabled, volunteering in a hospital, at a homeless shelter, or an agency that needs help, babysitting, caring for children, caring for the elderly, visiting people who are ill, making friends, going to parties, entertaining, going to amusement parks, tutoring, teaching English as a second language, etc.

5. Home & Family

People scoring high on this scale are interested in activities which allow them to be with other members of their family. Consider such leisure activities as baking pastries, cake decorating, hosting parties, sewing, cooking, cutting hair for family members, planning family recreational activities or vacations, traveling with family members if only for a weekend, shopping, attending children's school and athletic activities, watching sports, handling equipment for a local athletic team, serving family meals, teaching others how to cook or bake, canning and preserving food, cooking for community events, etc.

6. Technology

People scoring high on this scale are interested in anything related to technology and in designing, developing, managing, and supporting information systems. Consider such leisure activities as developing video games, participating in positive social media, robotics, programming, building websites, learning HTML, digital scrapbooking, social networking, photo editing, computer drawing, animation, blogging, graphic design, etc.

7. Mechanical

People scoring high on this scale are interested in using tools and machines to build, create, and repair things. They may enjoy working with their hands to develop products. Consider such leisure activities as fixing appliances, woodworking, home repairs, painting, repairing cars, auto body repair, wood carving, metal work, repairing watches and clocks, furniture repair, upholstery, model railroading, welding, car restoration, metalworking, candle making, leather working, etc.

8. Plants & Animals

People scoring high on this scale are interested in any activities that involve plants, animals, and natural resources. Consider such leisure activities as bird watching, riding horses, showing dogs, hiking, nature walks, hunting, fishing, camping, visiting state parks, flower arranging, animal breeding, pet watching, growing house plants, gardening, developing new plants by grafting from existing plants, playing with pets, landscaping, training pets, volunteering at a zoo, garden store, a pet store, etc.

These activities represent only a few options for each area of interest. There are many more! Research, talk to other people about their interests, and find additional alternative activities that will interest you and help you meet the same needs that gambling did! On the line below jot down some activities you think you would enjoy.

_____

_____

Exploring Better Alternatives

The best way to discontinue any type of gambling is to remove the elements necessary for gambling to occur in your life and replace them with healthier choices that will still meet your needs for excitement, stress reduction, overcoming boredom, etc.

*Identify some alternatives to gambling that you might like to pursue,
and how these alternatives will still meet your needs.*

1. EXAMPLE:

Alternatives to Gambling	My Needs Being Met
Walking more	*Reducing stress after work*
Hatchett Throwing for Sport	*Excitement*

NOW YOU TRY!

Alternatives to Gambling	My Needs Being Met

Managing Cravings

Cravings can be intense and they often feel as if they could last forever. An excellent way to approach gambling cravings is to pay attention to them, what they feel like, what you think about during the craving, and how long it tends to last. By studying the craving, you begin to take away its control over you.

Cravings often manifest themselves in your emotions (feeling irritable), behaviors (pacing), thoughts ("tonight I might win big and can quit!"), and bodily reactions (heart beating fast). If you are able to manage your cravings, you can find ways to stop gambling. As you build healthier choices, resisting cravings will become easier.

Ways to Overcome the Gambling Cravings When They Strike.

- Avoid isolation. By having a strong support network, you can call a trusted family member, meet a friend for a cup of coffee, or go to a Gamblers Anonymous meeting.
- Postpone gambling. Tell yourself that you'll wait five minutes, fifteen minutes, or an hour. As you wait, the urge to gamble may pass or become weak enough to resist. You may be able to become involved in something else.
- Visualization. Picture what might happen if you give in to the urge to gamble. Think about how you'll feel after all your money is gone and you've disappointed yourself and your family once again.
- Distract yourself. Engage immediately in another activity like going to the gym, watching a movie, or reading a great book.
- Relax. Practice relaxation exercises such as deep breathing, going for a walk, or exercising.

Complete the following table to explore your cravings and ways you will overcome the cravings.

When I Get the Cravings	How I Am Affected (Emotions, behaviors, thoughts, bodily reactions, etc.)	Ways to Overcome My Cravings
Example: When I am online and an ad for online poker pops up on my computer screen.	I have a shortness of breath and can feel my heart pounding!	I need to get my dog and go for a long walk.

Creating Healthy Habits

A very useful tip on how to stop gambling is to list the things you can and you want to do in your leisure time. It is important to make this leisure interest a habit that you can commit to daily, to ensure that you will have other choices if you have a craving to gamble.

In the spaces that follow, identify some of the activities you enjoy, and how you can make them a daily habit.

Leisure Activity	What I Like About It	How I Will Make it a Habit
Example: Painting.	*It is creative and allows me to be distracted, and attend to details.*	*I will work at my painting every day and I will be proud of myself.*

Here's how to ensure that something becomes a habit:

- Celebrate your small wins (and not by gambling!)
- Engage in the habit behavior every day.
- Have clear intentions.
- Start ridiculously small.
- Surround yourself with supporters.
- Use positive affirmations to maintain your motivation (I can do this!)
- Visualize your new habit.

Spending Time with Supportive People

Supportive people are those who provide emotional and practical help to someone who has an issue. They are people whom one can call on to spend leisure time and/or talk with, knowing that they will listen without judgment, and will offer good advice. These people are important in one's life when one is dealing with a gambling issue. Spending more time with people like this is one of the best alternatives to gambling. Who are people in your life who do not gamble, with whom you can spend time?

Below, identify those people and how you will begin spending more time with them.

Supportive People (USE NAME CODES)	Their Relationship to Me	How I Will Spend More Time With Them
Example: MKS	My children	Go to more of their sports events, concerts, movies, watch TV, etc.
Example: MAF	My aunt	She volunteers at a soup kitchen. I can ask if I can go with her.

Choose to focus your time, energy and conversation around people who inspire you, support you and help you to grow you into your happiest, strongest, wisest self.
~ Karen Salmansohn

Name three people in your life who can help you to grow you into your happiest, strongest, wisest self. Use a name code and briefly explain why you chose them.

1. _____

_____

2. _____

_____

3. _____

_____

© 2021 WHOLE PERSON ASSOCIATES, 101 WEST 2ND STREET, SUITE 203, DULUTH MN 55802 • 800-247-6789 • WHOLEPERSON.COM

Help Yourself by Helping Others

Volunteering is a great way to help others while helping yourself at the same time. Rather than engaging in gambling activities, you may want to consider volunteering to help others in your community. Volunteering allows you to engage in meaningful activities, find purpose in your life, and focus on something or someone outside of yourself.

Example: Delivering meals to people in need or helping at an animal shelter.

In the circles below, identify some of the places you might like to volunteer. Next to each, write why you would like this activity and how it would help you to deal with gambling issues.

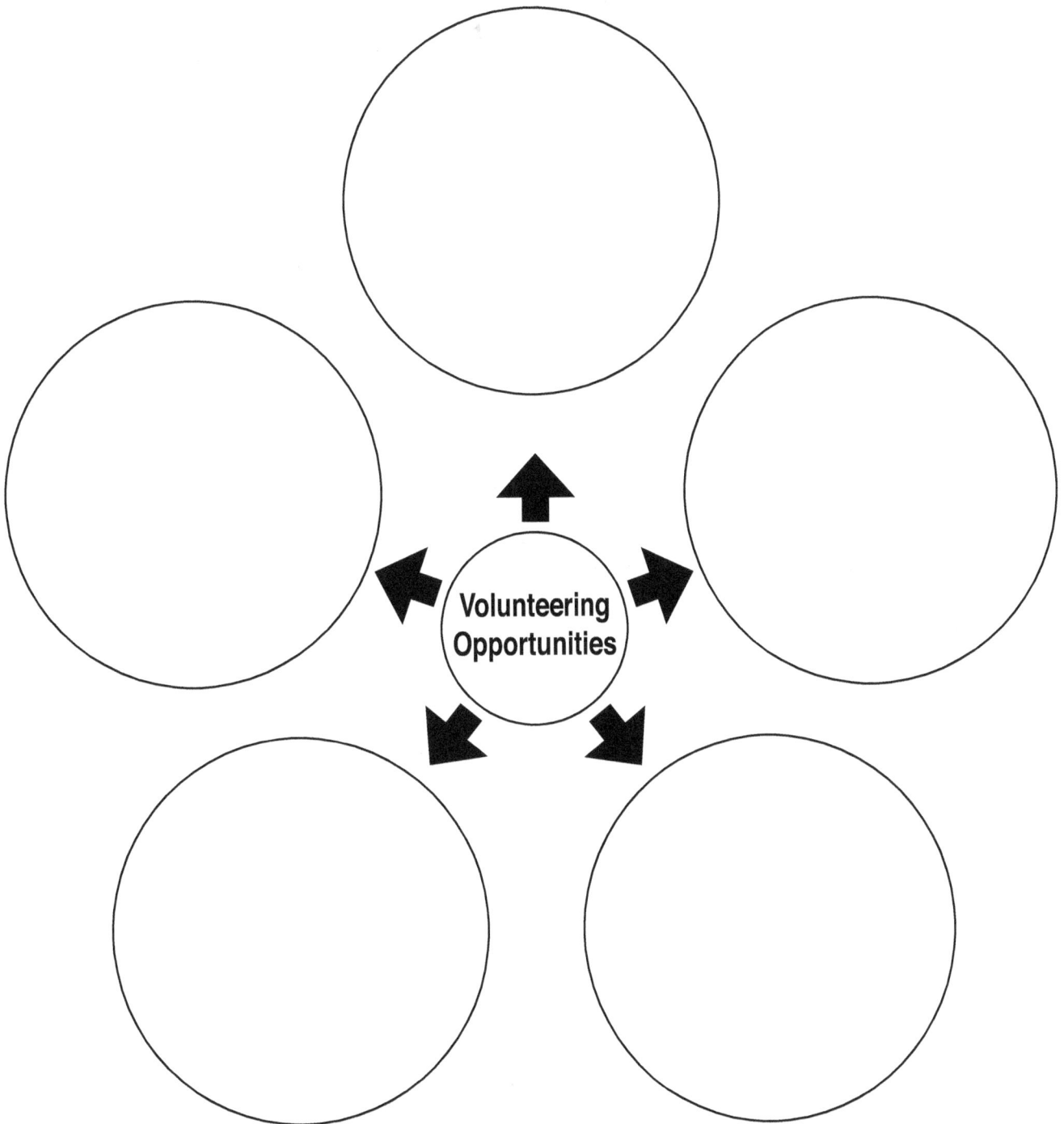

Volunteering Opportunities

Taking Time to Relax

It can be very difficult to give up gambling habits. Quitting after one has spent countless hours gambling of any kind can create tension and irritability – especially if one is losing! It is even worse when one encounters opportunities to gamble everywhere they turn, and bump into people who continue to gamble.

Learning how to relax can help you stick to your goal of overcoming your gambling habit.

Which of the following methods of relaxation below interest you?
For each one, write about how the method could relax you and how you might get involved in it.

Muscular relaxation (tensing and relaxing of all of the major muscles in your body in order from your head to your feet or feet to head)
Exercise (at a gym or at home)
Sports (playing or watching)
Yoga (a discipline which includes breath control, simple meditation, and the adoption of specific bodily postures)
Meditation (a technique for resting the mind and attaining a state of consciousness)
Walking, Jogging, Hiking, Power-walking (putting one step in front of the other leads to physical & mental benefits)
Spending time in nature (Stress reduction is one of the most well-known benefits of being in nature)
Other

© 2021 WHOLE PERSON ASSOCIATES, 101 WEST 2ND STREET, SUITE 203, DULUTH MN 55802 • 800-247-6789 • WHOLEPERSON.COM

How Does Gambling Affect You?

Lifestyle issues are important in dealing with a gambling addiction. When stressed, people who are addicted to gambling often neglect themselves!

Think about the ways you have taken care of yourself,
or have neglected to take care of yourself, while engaged in gambling.

Taking Care of Myself	How I React When Gambling	How I am Affected
Example: Food choices	*I don't care about eating when I am gambling.*	*I lost a huge amount of weight and got really ill!*
Example: Food choices	*I eat constantly when I am gambling.*	*I have become obese and my health is going downhill!*
Food Choces		
Exercise		
Sleep		
Relaxation		
Professional Help		
Spirituality		
Support		
Other		

Who are some trusted individuals that can help you to stop gambling, which would allow you to eat healthier, exercise, sleep better, relax, seek professional help, tap into your spiritual or religious side if you wish, and seek support and professional help?

Will you make a promise to contact this person or people? _____

Overcoming Loneliness

People who have a gambling issue often feel lonely and use gambling as a way of connecting with other people. Sometimes this connection is online and sometimes it is in person. It is important that you overcome your loneliness by getting involved with friends, family, and activities in your community, NOT with people who encourage your gambling! They are NOT friends. They don't like to gamble alone!

What types of social activities are offered in your community, local school or university, house of worship, fitness center, music groups, etc., that you might enjoy?

Possible Social Activities	How This Will Help Me	Steps I Will Take
Example: Have non-gambling get-togethers with my neighbors.	*I will be less lonely and this will give me something to do in the evenings.*	*I will start slow and ask a couple of neighbors over to my house to watch baseball. We won't bet!*

© 2021 WHOLE PERSON ASSOCIATES, 101 WEST 2ND STREET, SUITE 203, DULUTH MN 55802 • 800-247-6789 • WHOLEPERSON.COM

Dangerous Times Diary

The dangerous times for a person who is addicted are the times that they are susceptible to gambling. If you have been gambling for a while, you can see a pattern in your gambling habits. Once you can recognize your dangerous times you can make a plan to overcome it. The plan you build to find whys and ways to address the gambling problem will help you fight against the temptation from gambling.

To identify your dangerous times, journal in the diary page below.

Days of the Week	The type of gambling activities in which I engaged. The time and money I spent. Why I engaged in gambling. My thoughts, feelings and situations that occurred before and during the gambling session.
Sunday	
Monday	
Tuesday	
Wednesday	
Thursday	
Friday	
Saturday	

Copy this page and use it again and again to track your gambling activities.

Cool Activities I have Stopped Doing

When people are addicted to gambling, they don't realize it, but they slowly stop doing the things that used to interest them! It might be time for you to rethink the ways you fill your leisure time. Turning back to activities that you enjoyed in the past may require effort, but can be worthwhile, and may give you a replacement for gambling. This will boost your self-esteem and provide a non-gambling outlet.

Write, draw, or doodle some of the activities you have quit doing
and the people you miss being with but would consider starting again.

It is important to find healthy activities to replace your gambling addiction!

Taking Steps to Avoid Boredom

People with a gambling problem get bored easily and use this boredom as an excuse to gamble. When attempting to quit gambling, boredom can be a real issue.

To explore your ideas about filling in time when you get bored, complete the following sentence starters, then check off the items that sound interesting in the lower box.

The immediate thoughts that go through my head when I am bored are ...

When I struggle with boredom I usually ...

My favorite way to deal with boredom is ...

When I am not gambling, I can overcome my boredom by ...

When I become bored, I can ...

- ☐ Check out my ancestry.
- ☐ Clean closets.
- ☐ Create my own website.
- ☐ Drive somewhere I've never been.
- ☐ Experiment with a new recipe.
- ☐ Find a new podcast to listen to.
- ☐ Go for a hike somewhere I have not been.
- ☐ Invite people over.
- ☐ Join or watch a sports team.
- ☐ Look to adopt a pet (even if it is just a fish).
- ☐ Make an effort to learn something new.
- ☐ Plan a future trip.
- ☐ Plan a last-minute road trip.
- ☐ Plan a party.
- ☐ Reach out to a friend or relative I haven't seen in a while.
- ☐ Rearrange my furniture.
- ☐ Start a blog.
- ☐ Take a walk or hike out in nature or garden.
- ☐ Try learning a new language.
- ☐ Try out a new coffee shop.
- ☐ Try out a new restaurant.
- ☐ Visit a museum.
- ☐ Write a story of my life to hand down.

Major Goals & Mini-Goals

Your brain gets used to working in a certain way when gambling. When you try to stop, your brain still needs to be stimulated. It is important to set major goals and then mini-goals to make the major goals happen. When you are focused on your goals, you will be better able to cope with gambling urges that come your way.

Set a major goal that you have dreamed of achieving, then set some mini-goals that you can work on daily to reach your major goal.

Describe a major goal that you have dreamed of achieving (that is not related to gambling).

_____

_____

Think backwards and describe the mini-goals you would need to reach to achieve your major goal.

Example: My mini goals are:
1. *Decide on the subject and title.*
2. *What would the chapters be?*
3. *Who would the audience be...who would read it?*
4. *I need to find someone to mentor me.*
5. *Would I self-publish it?*
6. *Who would publish it?*
7. *When do I want to complete the book?*

My mini goals are:

1. _____

2. _____

3. _____

4. _____

5. _____

6. _____

7. _____

8. _____

9. _____

10. _____

Once you have completed your goal, start another one using the same process.

© 2021 WHOLE PERSON ASSOCIATES, 101 WEST 2ND STREET, SUITE 203, DULUTH MN 55802 • 800-247-6789 • WHOLEPERSON.COM

Running Away

Compulsive gambling is usually an attempt to satisfy some of your daily life demands. Some people gamble to feel stimulated while some others gamble to run away from mental stress, difficult people, depression, fatigue, and boredom.

What are you running from when you gamble?

Below, write about, draw, or doodle representations of what you run away from when you gamble. Be honest! No one needs to see your responses if you choose.

I AM RUNNING AWAY FROM ...	I AM RUNNING AWAY FROM ...
I AM RUNNING AWAY FROM ...	**I AM RUNNING AWAY FROM ...**

It's better to not be afraid of things and not avoid things.
~ Noomi Rapace

Rewarding Myself

It is important to remember to reward yourself when you avoid gambling activities! This will motivate you to duplicate this behavior even more. The challenge is to decide what reward would motivate you to reach your goal.

Your reward needs to be something that will give you the incentive to achieve your goal.
It needs to be within your budget and something you'll be excited about.

Consider possible rewards for non-gambling behavior:

- A reward that would be meaningful to me. _____

- A small reward I could give myself. _____

- A large reward I could give myself. _____

- A reward that would not cost money and would be fun. _____

- A reward I can afford and would be fun. _____

- A reward that I can enjoy alone. _____

- A reward I can enjoy with the people who support me. _____

Rewards are designed to help you pay attention to your triumphs, not your setbacks. Rewards will create good feelings and propel you to work harder on reaching your goals. Whenever you have completed or achieved one of your goals, treat yourself to one of the items on the list above. You can also reward yourself by giving yourself positive affirmations when achieving a goal.

Guidelines for creating positive affirmations include:
- *Make the affirmations positive and realistic.*
- *Create affirmations that appeal to you and nobody else.*
- *Repeat them as often as possible.*

Examples:
"I am stronger than my gambling addiction."
"I am going to overcome my gambling addiction."
"I am taking control of my life and my addiction."
"I am a happy and peaceful person."
"I will find energetic and/or relaxing alternatives."

Write your own affirmations in the boxes below and then transfer them onto sticky notes!

MY AFFIRMATIONS

Quotes about Finding Alternatives

On the lines that follow each of the quotations,
describe what the quotation means to you and how it applies to YOUR life.

Our greatest happiness does not depend on the condition of life in which
chance has placed us, but is always the result of a good conscience,
good health, occupation, and freedom in all just pursuits.
~ Thomas Jefferson

_____

_____

_____

All the money in the world can't buy you back good health.
~ Reba McEntire

_____

_____

_____

There are moments when all anxiety and stated toil are becalmed
in the infinite leisure and repose of nature.
~ Henry David Thoreau

_____

_____

_____

Boredom is your imagination calling to you.
~ Sherry Turkle

_____

_____

_____

WholePerson

Whole Person Associates is the leading publisher of training
resources for professionals who empower people to create and
maintain healthy lifestyles. Our creative resources will help
you work effectively with your clients in the areas
of stress management, wellness promotion,
mental health, and life skills.

Please visit us at our web site: **WholePerson.com**.
You can check out our entire line of products, place an order,
request our print catalog, and sign up for our monthly
special notifications.

Whole Person Associates
800-247-6789
Books@WholePerson.com